MY ANGRIA AND THE ANGRIANS

The Juvenilia Press Editions

The Juvenilia Press promotes the study of literary juvenilia, a category of literature that has been largely neglected. Its editions are slim volumes of early writings by children and adolescents (up to the approximate age of 20), including published and unpublished works of children: both those who achieved greatness as adults and those who did not become adult writers but whose writing is full of percipience and zest.

Founded in 1994 by Juliet McMaster at the University of Alberta in Edmonton, the Press has been based in the Faculty of Arts and Social Sciences at the University of New South Wales in Sydney since 2001, and has an international team of contributing editors from Britain, Canada, Japan, New Zealand, the United States, and Australia.

Each volume is devoted to a specific author and edited by an expert in the field, with the assistance of one or more students, usually postgraduates. Student involvement in the research and editorial process is an essential part of the pedagogic aim of the Juvenilia Press; and the illustrations, often executed by young aspiring artists or by the original young authors themselves, aim to capture the tone of the original productions. By contributing to the recovery, publication, and critical exploration of childhood writings, the Juvenilia Press actively promotes literary research and the professional development of students. At the same time, we endeavour to provide, for a wide audience, an insight into the creative energy of this rich and varied body of writing.

Christine Alexander
General Editor and Director

MY ANGRIA AND THE ANGRIANS

by Charlotte Brontë

Edited by Juliet McMaster, Leslie Robertson and the students of English 672 at the University of Alberta

with illustrations by Shannon Goetze

Introduction: Leslie Robertson
Textual editing: Astrid Blodgett, Carol-Ann Farkas, Jeffrey Herrle, Sherryl Maglione, Leslie Robertson
Annotations: Carol-Ann Farkas, Jeffrey Herrle, Douglas Lewis, Erin McLaughlin, Juliet McMaster, Leslie Robertson, Barbara Simler, Robert Summers
"'The Best Book' and This Book": Douglas Lewis

Juvenilia Press

My Angria and the Angrians
ISBN: 0-9681961-0-1

First published 1997
Reprinted Sydney, Australia 2011

Cover Drawing: Shannon Goetze
Cover and Interior Design: Winston Pei / Black Riders Design

CONTENTS

MAPS

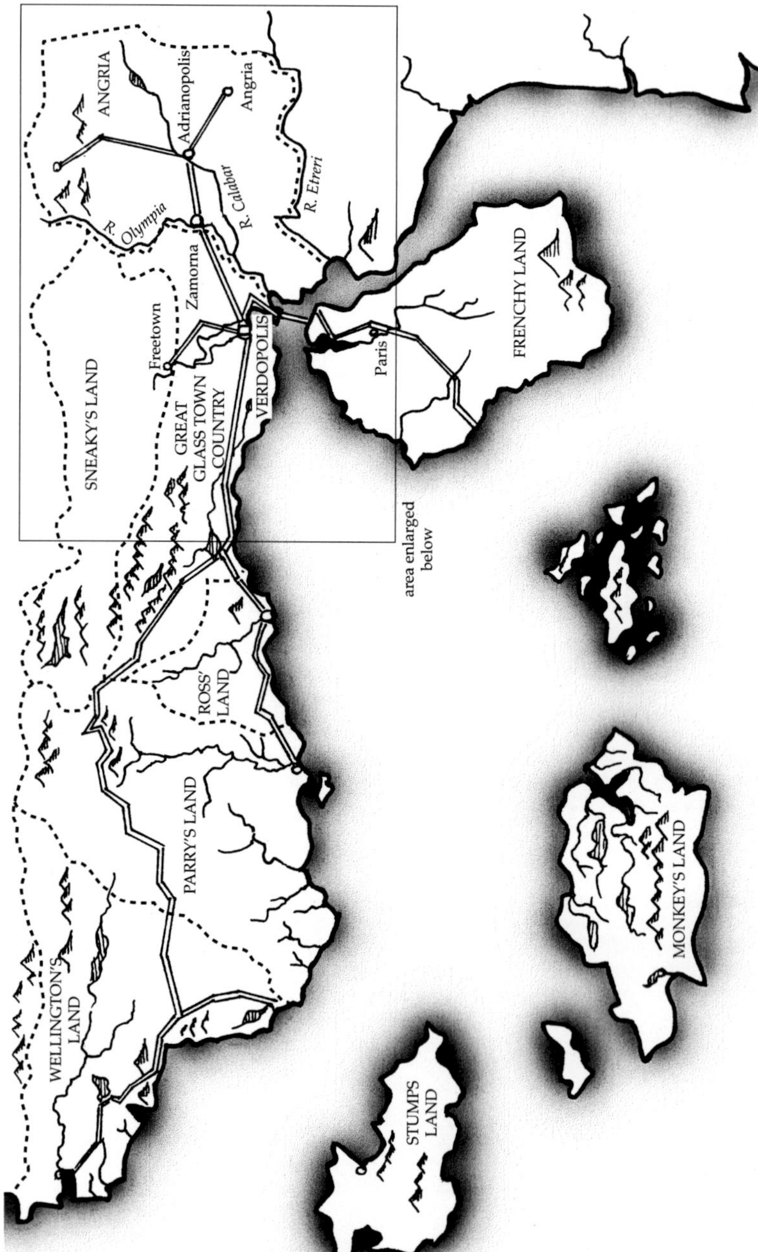

THE GREAT GLASS TOWN FEDERATION, AND ANGRIA

Based on Branwell Brontë's frontispiece to The History of the Young Men *(1830-31), with Angria added.*

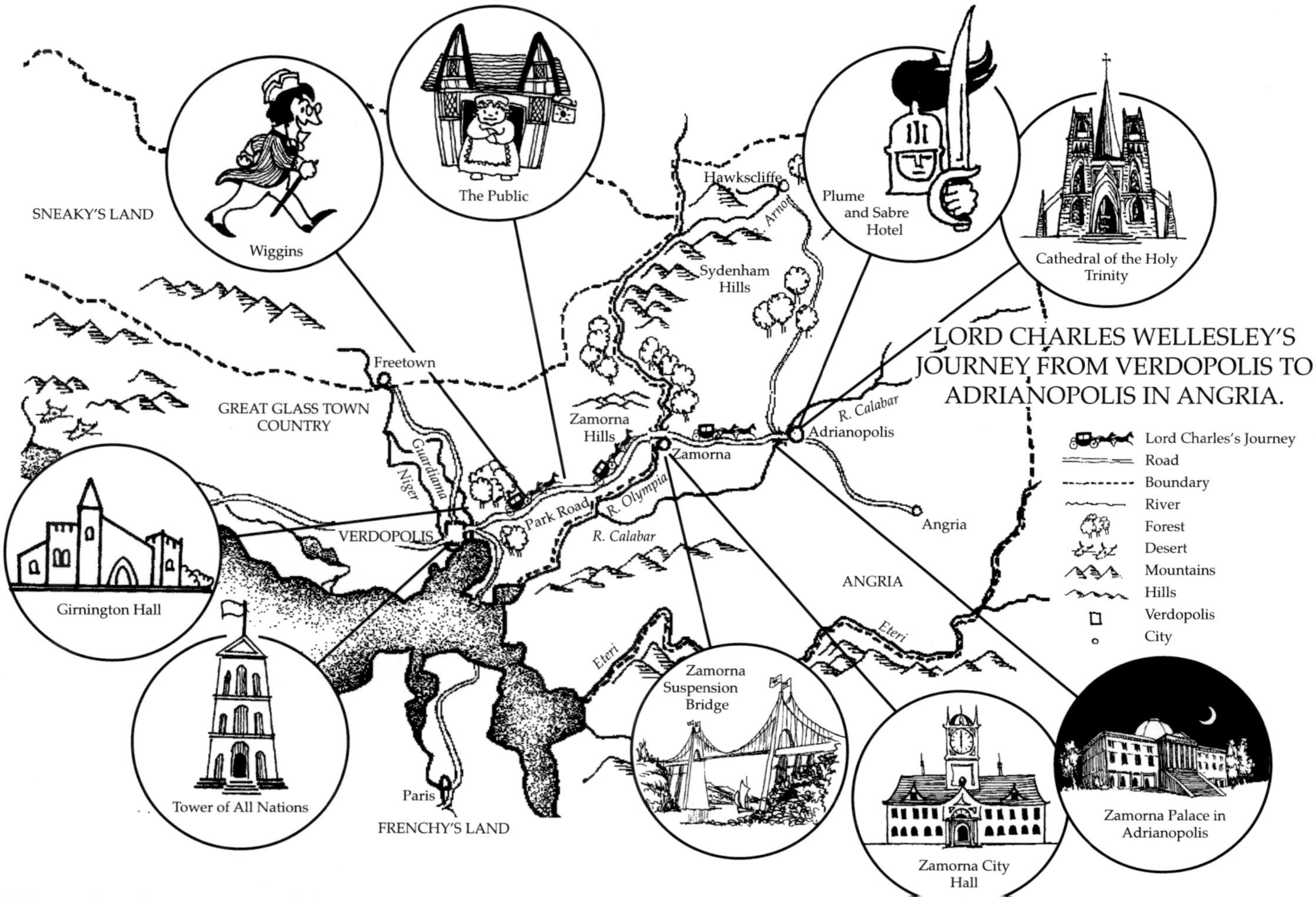
LORD CHARLES WELLESLEY'S JOURNEY FROM VERDOPOLIS TO ADRIANOPOLIS IN ANGRIA.
Lord Charles's Journey
Road
Boundary
River
Forest
Desert
Mountains
Hills
Verdopolis
City
SNEAKY'S LAND
Wiggins
The Public
Plume and Sabre Hotel
Cathedral of the Holy Trinity
Hawkscliffe
R. Arnor
Sydenham Hills
Freetown
GREAT GLASS TOWN COUNTRY
Zamorna Hills
Zamorna
Adrianopolis
R. Calabar
Guardiama
Niger
Park Road
R. Olympia
VERDOPOLIS
R. Calabar
Angria
ANGRIA
Eteri
Eteri
Girnington Hall
Tower of All Nations
Paris
FRENCHY'S LAND
Zamorna Suspension Bridge
Zamorna City Hall
Zamorna Palace in Adrianopolis

PREFACE

Angria, with its national colour of red, and its national symbol of the rising sun, its victorious monarch and its cheering populace, typifies the "infernal world" that Charlotte and Branwell Brontë created in their youthful fictions. In Angria everything is over the top. In developing this new region of the Great Glass Town Confederacy, Charlotte could give rein to her imagination, and turn her cramped world of Haworth parsonage into a kingdom fabulously rich, run by a king stunningly attractive, supported by an aristocracy shamelessly self-indulgent. When this kingdom needs an heir, the queen produces not just a baby, not just a boy, but twin boys, "in the right, good, dashing Angrian style," as the young narrator reflects. "Angria will have nothing trite. There must be flash and bustle and rising sunism about all her affairs."

But this story of the far-away kingdom is also enlivened by some close reference to the Haworth home front. Among the pilgrims on the exodus from Verdopolis towards Angria is one Patrick Wiggins, Charlotte's caricature of Branwell. The "low, slightly built man," with his spectacles and "bush of carroty hair," is Charlotte's revenge on her turbulent brother, who in his turn pours scorn on his sisters, Charlotte, "a broad dumpy thing," Emily, "lean and scant," and Anne, who is "nothing, absolutely nothing." A little mayhem among siblings has its own appeal.

An edition of *My Angria and the Angrians* thus offers itself as a natural choice for the Juvenilia Press, which specializes in publishing the early works of known writers. Charlotte wrote it in 1834, when she was eighteen: and since it comes relatively late among the burgeoning fictions of Verdopolis, it provides a chance to draw them together and epitomise them. We intend our edition to be both an example of the Brontës' extraordinary sagas, and a guide to them. Hence we provide maps, family trees, introduction, illustrations, and ample explanatory annotation, as well as the narrative itself.

Young members of the Brontë Society have taken the appropriate name of the Young Angrians. Here is their model, in the vivid doings of the original Angrians!

J.M.

INTRODUCTION

> *...[A]t eighteen the true narrative of life is yet to be commenced. Before that time, we sit listening to a tale, a marvellous fiction; delightful sometimes, and sad sometimes; almost always unreal. Before that time, our world is heroic; its inhabitants half-divine or semi-divine; its scenes are dream-scenes: darker woods, and stranger hills; brighter skies, more dangerous waters; sweeter flowers, more tempting fruits; wider plains, drearier deserts, sunnier fields than are found in nature, overspread our enchanted globe. What a moon we gaze on before that time! How the trembling of our hearts at her aspect bears witness to its unutterable beauty! As to our sun, it is a burning heaven — the world of gods.* (Shirley 121)

Charlotte Brontë was herself just eighteen years old when she wrote *My Angria and the Angrians* in 1834. Perhaps she was remembering the "marvellous fiction" of her own juvenile writings when she wrote the above words in her 1849 novel *Shirley*. Certainly the description applies to her own juvenilia, written chiefly between 1829 when she was thirteen and 1839 when she was twenty-three. *My Angria and the Angrians*, the example offered here, provides an excellent example of the range of emotion and technique to be found in the juvenilia. Here we have the high drama of Zamorna's tortured relationship with his wife juxtaposed with the high comedy of Patrick Benjamin Wiggins, a caricature of Branwell Brontë, and his absurdly pompous speeches. The political drama surrounding the birth of twin heirs to Zamorna is coupled with the political satire of Charles Warner's speech at the hustings. At times the text takes on the character of "a medley of glimpses of life in Zamorna's new kingdom" (*An Edition of the Early Writings of Charlotte Brontë* II.ii.xv[1]).

What unity it has is chiefly provided by the voice of its first-person narrator, Lord Charles Albert Florian Wellesley, still a child at the time of this story. His youth provides some explanation for the apparent ease with which he eavesdrops on the conversations he reports to us. This seems to be the case on the memorable evening he spends with Major Albert Howard and his companions at Elm Grove Villa, for example (27-8). At other times it is his rank and relationship to Zamorna that give him access to private conversations, as when he follows Major Howard into the palace: "I followed, of course opposed by neither the sentinel nor Eugene, both happening to be well acquainted with me" (30). Sometimes, however, there seems no plausible explanation for Lord Charles' presence at a scene. Christine Alexander's summation of his role in *Something About Arthur* (1833) as "often awkward and inappropriate" at times applies equally well to this tale: "Because Charlotte fails to observe the limitations of the first person narrator, Lord Charles becomes an implausible character, crouching under tables and behind locked doors in order to be able to overhear and later repeat conversations. He is omniscient and omnipresent..." (Alexander [1983] 226). Too often, as well, his voice is not that of a child; indeed, the first-time reader may not even realise that he is one. The young Charlotte Brontë is in love with language and is often not willing to sacrifice a fine effect to the demands of mere realism. She was later to gain from these early experiments in telling a story from the point of view of a child narrator in the early chapters of *Jane Eyre*. The more realistic scenes in *My Angria* are almost invariably comic. Lord Charles' encounter with Wiggins has already been noted, as has Charles Warner's wonderfully funny speech at the hustings, which is remarkably prescient of the speech-giving scenes early in Dickens' *The Pickwick Papers* (1836-7). Another such moment closes the story, as Lord Charles abruptly ends his narration by accidentally falling out of a window (59).

The existence of the Brontë juvenilia was first brought to public attention in 1857 with the publication of Mrs. Gaskell's *The Life of Charlotte Brontë*. "I have had a curious packet confided to me," she wrote, "containing an immense amount of manuscript, in an inconceivably small space...in a hand which it is almost impossible to decipher without the aid of a magnifying glass" (Gaskell 64). It was she, too, who first quoted Charlotte's account in "The History of the Year" (1829) of the origins of what would eventually become the Angrian and Gondal sagas:

> Papa brought Branwell some soldiers from Leeds. When Papa came home it was night and we were in bed, so next morning Branwell came to our door with a box of soldiers. Emily and I jumped out of bed and I snatched up one and exclaimed, "This is the Duke of Wellington! It shall be mine!" When I said this, Emily likewise took one and said it should be hers. When Anne came down she took one also. Mine was the prettiest of the whole and perfect in every part. Emily's was a grave-looking fellow. We called him "Gravey." Anne's was a queer little thing, very much like herself. He was called "Waiting Boy." Branwell chose "Bonaparte" (*ECB* I.5).

"Gravey" and "Waiting Boy" clearly "did not stand a chance in the glamour of a heroic fairy-tale world," Christine Alexander has noted, and so "[t]heir feeble names were soon exchanged for those of Parry and Ross, two famous explorers and more suitable companions for Wellington and Bonaparte" (Alexander [1983] 27-8).

Although the sagas of Angria and Gondal (written by Charlotte and Branwell, Emily and Anne respectively) have their roots in the tales woven around these characters, this is clearly not the first occasion on which the children had amused themselves by the making up of stories. "The Origin of the O'Deans" (1829), for example, refers briefly to a similar act of group story-telling:

> The origin of the O'Deans was as follows: we pretended we had each a large island inhabited by people six miles high. The people we took out of Aesop's *Fables*. Hay Man was my chief man, Boaster Branwell's, Hunter Anne's and Clown Emily's. Our chief men were ten miles high except Emily's who was only four. (*ECB* I.6)

This short paragraph is one of the only extant manuscripts relating to "Our Fellows' Play," to which Charlotte briefly refers in "The History of the Year" (*ECB* I.5). Although "Our Fellows' Play" was to leave little mark on the Glass Town saga (from which was to develop in turn the Angrian and Gondal cycles), this fragment—with its passing reference to Aesop—is a reminder of the importance of the children's reading to their writing.

Books were important in the Brontë household. The children's father was an educated and well-read man with a passion for literature. The "indescribable pleasure" he gained from writing" (Alexander [1983] 13) resulted in the publication of several books between 1811 and 1820. Alexander speculates that his "publications, regardless of literary merit, were early incentives in making his children writers" (Alexander [1983] 14). Another incentive was the intense affection between Charlotte and her siblings; Mrs. Gaskell describes it as "stronger than either death or life" (Gaskell 128). Their unusual closeness "may help to account for the intense passion with which the young Brontës pursued their joint creative ventures" (Alexander [1983] 12). As Alexander has written, "It is not unusual for siblings to recite stories to each other; it is less common to record them on scraps of paper and to take such care with their execution" (Alexander [1983] 11). The first surviving example of Charlotte Brontë's writing ("There was once a little girl and her name was Ane" [1826] *ECB* I.3) shows with what seriousness she already took both her writing and the material production of books; it is carefully written, lovingly illustrated, and sewn together to form a booklet with a cover made from a scrap of patterned wallpaper. In its careful presentation and its tiny size (only 3.6 X 5.6 cm) this early manuscript is typical of the later Brontë juvenilia.

The children's early reading naturally played a great role in their writing.[2] Mrs. Gaskell lists some of the works to which they would have been exposed:

> Up and down the house, were to be found many standard works of a solid kind. Sir Walter Scott's writings, Wordsworth's and Southey's poems were among the lighter literature; while, as having a character of their own—earnest, wild, and occasionally fanatical—may be named some of the books which came from the Branwell side of the family—from the Cornish followers of the saintly John Wesley—and which are touched on in the account of the works to which Caroline Helstone had access in "Shirley":—"Some venerable Lady's Magazines,...some mad Methodist Magazines full of miracles and apparitions, and preternatural warnings, ominous dreams, and frenzied fanaticism; and the equally mad letters of Mrs Elizabeth Rowe from the Dead to the Living." (Gaskell 97-98)

Winifred Gérin includes among her list of "the books that had most impressed" the Brontë children "*Aesop's Fables, The Arabian Nights,* the *Travels of Mungo Park,* the Arctic voyages of William Parry and Sir John Ross, the novels of Scott, the poetry of Byron, translations from Chateaubriand's works, . . . and Southey's instantly popular *History of the Peninsular War* (1823-32)" (Gérin I.19). Mr. Brontë made every effort to provide a wide range of reading material for them, buying as many books as he could with his limited means and joining the Keighley Mechanics' Institute soon after it was founded in 1825 so that the family could borrow books from its library (Alexander [1983] 20). One must also bear in mind the family's passionate interest in politics and current events. In "The History of the Year" Charlotte says that they "take 2 and see three newspapers a week. We take the *Leeds Intelligencer,* party Tory, and the *Leeds Mercury,* Whig, edited by Mr. Baines and his brother, son-in-law and his 2 sons, Edward and Talbot. We see the *John Bull;* it is a High Tory, very violent. Mr. Driver lends us it, as likewise *Blackwoods Magazine,* the most able periodical there is" (*ECB* I.4). All of this contributed to what Gérin calls "the absolute intellectual freedom of their home" (Gérin I.9).

The passionate nature of the family's interest in politics is made evident in an oft-quoted passage from "Tales of the Islanders, Volume II" (1829):

> I remember the day when the *Intelligence Extraordinary* came with Mr Peel's speech in it, containing the terms on which the Catholics were to be let in. With what eagerness Papa tore off the cover, and how we all gathered round him, and with what breathless anxiety we listened, as one by one they were disclosed and explained and argued upon so ably and so well. (*ECB* I.100)

Her interest in politics, fostered in childhood, did not leave her as she grew older; on 13 March 1835 she wrote to her friend Ellen Nussey:

> What do you think of the course Politics are taking? I make this inquiry because I now think you have a wholesome interest in the matter; formerly you did not care greatly about it. (Shorter I.114)

Charlotte's own "wholesome interest" in politics and the affairs of the wider world beyond Haworth is evident from a very early date in her juvenilia. In "The origin of the Islanders" (1829) she describes how she and her siblings amused themselves "one wet night in December" :

> [A]t last I said, "Suppose we had each an Island of our own." Branwell chose the Isle of Man, Emily Isle of Arran and Bute Isle, Anne, Jersey, and I chose the Isle of Wight. We then chose who should live in our Islands. The chief of Branwell's were John Bull, Astley Cooper, Leigh Hunt, etc.; Emily's Walter Scott, Mr Lockhart, Johnny Lockhart etc.; Anne's Michael Sadler, Lord Bentinck, Henry Halford, etc.; and I chose Duke of Wellington and son, North and Co.; 30 officers, Mr Abernathy, etc. (*ECB* I.6)

As Christine Alexander notes in her annotations to this passage in *An Edition of the Early Writings of Charlotte Brontë,* the names were chiefly those of famous men of the period. "Politics," says Mrs. Gaskell, "was evidently their grand interest; the Duke of Wellington their demi-god" (Gaskell 72). A similar mixture of the fantastic and the real characterises all Charlotte's early writings.

The real, contemporary world she knew chiefly through her reading affects the choice of place-names in the juvenilia, as well. A modern critic has described how the maps and information provided in Goldsmith's *Grammar of General Geography* "were used to give the imaginary countries of Angria and Gondal a local habitation and a name" (Williams 30). Angria abounds in place-names reminiscent of England; examples from *My Angria and the Angrians* alone include Northangerland, York Place, Thorncliffe, Howard, the Black Bull public house, Stuartville Road, Arundel, Humeshire, and Hawkescliffe Forest. Some of these are associated with the Brontë family. Howard, for example, is meant to recall Haworth, the Yorkshire village in which Mr. Brontë was parson. In *My Angria and the Angrians* Patrick Benjamin Wiggins sings its praises in extravagant terms:

> 'I always account myself a native of Howard, a great city among the Warner Hills, under the dominion of that wonderful and superhuman gentleman Warner Howard Warner, Esqr' (here he took off his hat and bowed low). 'It has four churches and above twenty grand hotels, and a street called the Taan Gate, far wider than Bridgenorth in Free Town.' (9)

This grand description of the town is comically at variance with the real Haworth, which one modern literary historian has described as "one of the unhealthiest small towns in England" (Wilks 35). Wiggins's one-man audience, the tale's narrator Charles Wellesley, knows just how much credence he should grant to such extravagant assertions:

> 'None of your humbug, Wiggins,' said I. 'I know well enough Howard is only a miserable little village, buried in dreary moors and moss-hags and marshes. I question whether it has one church or anything nearer an hotel than that wayside ale-house you are now eyeing so longingly.' (9-10)

The joking reference to the ale-house reminds the reader that Branwell was indeed a regular customer at such places, especially at the Black Bull in Haworth, which stood hard by the church and parsonage. In 1834, when Branwell was only seventeen, his drinking was still a matter for jesting; it was not to remain so.

But the recurrent use of English place-names in the African land of Angria is more than a literary curiosity; it is a reminder that Angria is in fact a colony. In "The Twelve Adventurers," one of the earliest of Charlotte's extended stories (dated 15 April 1829),[3] she describes how "twelve men from Britain of a most gigantic size" sailed forth "on the 1st of March 1793" (*ECB* I.8-9). Among this band was Arthur Wellesley, later to be Duke of Wellington and father of Arthur—Marquis of Douro, Duke of Zamorna, and King of Angria—and Charles, who was to become the most important of Charlotte's pseudonyms. After a series of adventures these twelve men arrive on the coast of Africa, where they immediately engage in battle with the natives:

> The Chief then said, "Who are you?"
> Wellesley answered, "We were cast up on your shores by a storm and request shelter."
> They said, "You shall not have any."
> Wellesley: "We will take it then!"
> We prepared for battle; they did the same.
> It was a very fierce encounter, but we conquered. (*ECB* I.10)

In these terse sentences the narrator betrays attitudes not unrelated to those that allowed Britain to conquer half the globe. One must remember that the nineteenth century was a period of tremendous imperial expansion and that Africa was one important theatre for that expansion. Although the partition of Africa by the European powers took place largely after 1870, British activity on the continent was already widespread during the first decades of the nineteenth century (Williamson II.174), and British confidence in the legitimacy of such activity was perhaps at its height during this period. Although many historians of empire centre their discussions around the final decades of the nineteenth century, "[a] closer look at the cultural actuality reveals a much earlier, more deeply and stubbornly held view about overseas European hegemony; we can locate a coherent, fully mobilised system of ideas near the end of the eighteenth century" (Said [1993] 58). The Brontë children were, in large measure, the products of that system, as *My Angria and the Angrians* demonstrates. To say this is neither to condemn nor dismiss their work. As Edward Said has written, "in studying cultural texts that happily co-existed with or lent support to the global enterprises of European and American empire, one is not indicting them wholesale or suggesting that they are less interesting as art for being in complex ways part of the imperialist undertaking" (Said [1993] 186). Rather, the attempt to explore their position in history increases their interest for both reader and critic.

The Chief whom the adventurers take prisoner in "The Twelve Adventurers" identifies his country as "Ashantee," a name made familar to the English by newspaper reports of the Ashantee Wars in the 1820s (Meyer 159). After accepting the natives' proposal of peace, offered "on terms the most advantageous to ourselves" (*ECB* I.11), the conquerors—still only twelve in number—set about building a city with supernatural aid. As Arthur Wellesley later says to his companions,

> But in what a short time have we built [the city] we now are in! How long has it taken to rear the Grand Hall where we now are? Have not these marble pillars and that solemn dome been built by supernatural power? If you view the city from this Gothic window and see the beams of the morn gilding the battlements of the mighty towers, and the pillars of the splendid palaces which have been reared in a few months, can you doubt that magic has been used in their construction? (*ECB* I.13)

Thus, it seems, all the forces of the earth—both natural and supernatural—join together to ensure the success of the British colonising efforts.

They aid also in the defeat of the native population: "Now, if the genii have built us our city," continues Arthur Wellesley (soon to be declared by the same genii Duke of Wellington), "will they not likewise help us against the assaults of the enemy?" (*ECB* I.13). And so they do, although the Englishmen hardly seem to need their help, so negligible is the threat of native victory over them made to seem: "For about ten years after this we continued at war with the blacks, and then made peace; after which, for about ten years more, nothing happened worth mentioning" (*ECB* I.16). By 1827 the wonders of the city, its population grown to fifteen thousand, include a Grand Inn "which was a most superior building and large enough to accommodate 20,000 men" (*ECB* I.17-8). Clearly the colony is prospering. On 14 June of that year "a council of the whole nation was summoned" and the Duke of Wellington—now become "the conqueror of Bonaparte and the deliverer of Europe" (*ECB* I.17)—is proclaimed king (*ECB* I.18). As well as being a basic fact of the juvenilia, colonialism also plays a part in the mature novels, as the critic Susan Meyer has argued: "In both *Shirley* (1849) and *Villette* (1853), the men with whom the heroines are in love either leave or threaten to leave Europe for places of European colonisation, and both men imagine their relationships with colonised people as standing in for their relationships with white women" (Meyer 159). Such images and motifs of Charlotte's mature novels have deep roots in her juvenilia.

This easy acceptance by a Yorkshire teenager of Britain's imperialistic ventures provides remarkable evidence of the cultural force that lay behind the phenomenon. Edward Said has written that, in nineteenth-century Europe, "scarcely a corner of life was untouched by the facts of empire" (Said [1993] 8). Setting the Angrian stories in Africa, therefore, cannot be seen as a politically inert choice by the author. "To represent Africa is to enter into the battle over Africa" (Said [1993] 68). While this may seem to overstate the political engagement of such a young woman, it is important not only to remember Charlotte Brontë's intense interest in politics and current events, but also to see her work in the context of her culture. British imperialism in the nineteenth century was made possible by a complex network of cultural forces, literature among them. "References to Australia in *David Copperfield* or India in *Jane Eyre*," Said asserts, "are made because they *can be*, because British power (and not just the novelist's fancy) made passing references to these massive appropriations possible" (Said [1993] 66). A similar claim can be made for the Angrian stories: they are placed in Africa because they can be, because an entire ideological and cultural structure makes such massive fictional appropriations possible. The fact that the influence of that network of cultural forces is so evident in the work of an isolated teenager is further evidence of its force.

In *My Angria and the Angrians*, one can see these cultural systems at work in interesting ways. While the colony established on the coast of Africa has clearly been very successful for many years, it is ready to move on to a new stage in its existence: the establishment of the kingdom of Angria under the leadership of Zamorna. A new and glorious national capital has been constructed, and the ruler of this kingdom now sets about consolidating his power. The construction of the capital city has been a major undertaking, but the real work—that of constructing the nation itself in the hearts and minds of its inhabitants—is a greater work still. If, as Benedict Anderson writes, the nation may be defined as an "imagined political community" (Anderson 6), then both the form of the narrative and its content are here engaged in a similarly creative act; the creation of both narrative and nation spring from the same source. It is with this narration of nation-building that *My Angria and the Angrians* is chiefly concerned. In describing this process, Charlotte Brontë naturally draws on what she knows.

In many ways, the nation of Angria seems very English. As always in the Brontë juvenilia, the names of its most notable inhabitants read like a jumbled roll call of English historical figures and great families: Percy, Seymour, Wellesley, Sydney, Castlereagh, Wellington, Stanhope, and Arundel; such names are evocative of an heroic national past. Wiggins frequents the Black Bull public house (13) and drinks tea, ale, and porter while eating cheese and cold beef (10) for all the world as if he were in a novel by Dickens. The Englishness of *My Angria and the Angrians* goes deeper than such details, however. The celebration of the nation of Angria is modelled in many ways on that of Great Britain.

Linda Colley has described Great Britain as "an invented nation superimposed...onto much older alignments and loyalties" (Colley 5) which stood in need of a conscious programme of patriotic celebration in order to create a sense of national identity among its people. Angria, too, is a country only recently established and therefore in need of definition and celebration; in fact, *My Angria and the Angrians* is the first work in which "the full influence of Angria is felt in Charlotte's writing" (Alexander [1983] 122), as it had been founded only months before in her work and in Branwell's. One element of national celebration in this tale that provides an interesting point of comparison to that of Great Britain is the use of music. It was only in the early 1800s that "God Save the King" came to be called the national anthem, a term the British invented (Colley 44). Angria, too, has a "grand national anthem," entitled "Sound the loud trumpets o'er Afric's dark sea"; it is a "sublime song with a sound so loud, so full, so deep in its cadences, so triumphant in its swells, that it seemed as if the thunders sung in heaven, and the winds and seas of earth made answer to them" (22).

The one composer mentioned by name in *My Angria* is Handel (13), the very composer described by Colley as "a national institution" for his glowing celebration of Britain (Colley 32). One of Handel's tasks was the composition of music suitable for occasions of national importance, such as the coronation ode written for George II in 1727. A similar role is played by the unnamed composer[4] of "Hurrah for the Gemini!" on the occasion of the birth of twin heirs to Zamorna, ruler of Angria. The words of that song celebrate the new nation:

> Sons of an imperial line!
> Welcome to your land and home!
> Not at daylight's dark decline
> Princes! is your advent come ...
> But at morning's prima; flush,

> Angria's bright, uprising day,
> When her hills have caught the blush
> Of the earliest, fairest ray. (54)

The words also create the image of the nation as a natural phenomenon, made not by man but by God, thus recalling the aid of the genii in *The Twelve Adventurers* in causing the colony's first city, Glass Town, to rise from the African wilderness:

> With your God-like father's form
> Catch his spirit, catch his might,
> Then, albeit the battle-storm
> Gather round us black as night,
> Still its blasts we may defy,
> Still our flag aloft shall fly,
> Still shall Angria's burning sky
> Smile its living light. (55)

Such words echo the eighteenth- and nineteenth-century sense of great Britain as a nation peculiarly blessed by God (Colley 32) and destined by Him to prosper (Colley 43).

The cause of the great national celebrations which close *My Angria and the Angrians* is the birth of twin boys, heirs to the newly established kingdom. The rejoicings of the people at this event are fervent:

> The crowds were actually convulsed with enthusiasm at this intelligence. I left them, darkening the sun with their headgear, leaping, roaring, and hurrahing like mad. . . . [All] revelled in a storm of glorious confusion; messengers returning and going forth; orders issuing for universal rejoicings; for the opening of hotels and ale-houses at His Majesty's expense. (50)

Such public celebrations of a dynastic event recall those of an earlier age in England. Upon the birth of the future Edward VI in October 1537, for example, there were rejoicings throughout the realm, especially in London, where bonfires were lit, bells rung, banners and garlands hung, salvos fired, and "every conduit gushed ale or wine, and families sat round them on empty hogsheads, eating, drinking, lurching up to dance and kiss each other, crying, laughing, bawling out choruses from the broadsheets that had been printed weeks before" (Chapman 27). By creating a scene that might have come out of English history, Charlotte Brontë essentially brings the past and the present of the nation together, creating thereby a sense of history for a nation still too new to have its own. As one critic has noted in a discussion of nationalism and literary form, reading the nation backwards into history in this way places it "in an 'immemorial past' where its arbitrariness cannot be questioned" (Brennan 45).

As numerous as the suggestions of Englishness (or, rather, Britishness) are, however, the reader of *My Angria and the Angrians* cannot help but notice the atmosphere of exoticism that also pervades the text. A few examples will suffice to establish the motif: the city is compared to Babylon (2), Lady Julia resides in her "Eastern Paradise" (4), Wiggins falls on his face, "prostrated towards the east like a Parsee worshipping the new risen sun" and regrets not having thrown himself beneath the wheels of Edward Percy's coach "like a Hindoo beneath the car of Juggernaut" (8-9), Georgiana and Eliza Seymour sit "with the grace and air of Persian princesses" (22), and Mary Henrietta's apartments are a vision of Oriental splendour:

> Here warm lights were glowing over the rich deep sombre hangings, dazzling carpets, and Tyrian couches. Queen Mary Henrietta appeared in the midst alone, alone (as Julia Sydney says), partially reclined on the piled cushions of a purple silk ottoman, beautiful, delicate as a dream, all fair and soft and tranquil and imperial. (31)

As Edward Said has argued, the development of academic and popular Orientalism had made a construction of the mysterious, opulent East widely available to both readers and writers of the nineteenth century (Said [1979] 52). Charlotte Brontë's most direct experience of this would have been through the Oriental tales of Byron (whose influence on her has been well documented [Zonana 594]), the *Arabian Nights*, and Sir Charles Morell's *Tales of the Genii* (Alexander [1983] 18). The nation of Angria is both familiarly English and exotically foreign,[5] both known and unknown. It thus combines her reading and her experience as a British subject.

During the painfully lonely years Charlotte spent as a teacher at Roe Head school (1835-8), the secret (to all but her family) dreamworld of Angria and the pleasure she took in it increasingly became a source of concern for her. "Angria," Christine Alexander writes, "had become a furtive substitute for reality, an obsession about which Charlotte began to feel guilty" (Alexander [1980] 56). The security she had once found in the "self-referential world of the imagination" (Alexander [1991] 189) was now lost in her sense of confusion and loss of control. In the later juvenilia she attempts to regain control over "the fantastic, the violent, and the perversely morbid in her stories by concentrating instead on minute fidelity to realistic detail" (Blom 292). This effort is already apparent in *My Angria and the Angrians*, particularly in the scenes with Wiggins. Here, both language (though Wiggins's is comically extravagant) and landscape are closer to the world she knows by experience. Still, her "attempts to domesticate her imagination failed to eliminate violence and perversity from what she guiltily referred to as 'the world below'" (Blom 293). As her struggle intensifies, her dreamworld descends into civil war (which M.A. Blom calls "the objective correlative of the fragmented self," being "emblematic of and stemming from ambivalent and mutually destructive internal impulses" [294]). The civil war takes on a distinctly familial aspect: Percy, Zamorna's father-in-law and prime minister, leads a rebellion against him, and Quashia, the African native who was raised as Zamorna's foster brother, leads an invasion that threatens to drive the long-established colonists out of Africa altogether. After her "Farewell to Angria" (1839), there comes a long gap before she writes *The Professor* in 1846. The "'plain and homely' realism" of this, her first novel, shows a marked change in style from "the 'ornamented and redundant composition' of her Angrian stories" (Alexander [1980] 57). During the intervening years, she had struggled to break away from the imaginary world to which she was drawn like an addict to opium (Alexander [1980] 56), to cast off both the style and the subject matter of her juvenilia and "turn her talents to practical—in other words, publishable—account" (Blom 292). This struggle was to bear fruit in the remarkable and instantly popular *Jane Eyre*. Reading Charlotte Brontë's juvenilia, therefore, is useful not only for the glimpses it affords of the mature writer in embryo, but also for the evidence it offers of a long struggle to bring a powerful imagination under control. *My Angria and the Angrians*, it is hoped, will give the reader something to ponder on both these fronts, while providing its own, very real reading pleasure.

NOTES FOR THE INTRODUCTION

1 Subsequent references to this edition of Charlotte Brontë's juvenilia will use the initials *ECB* followed by the volume and page numbers.

2 A brief account of the evidence of Charlotte Brontë's early reading to be found in her mature works is in F.B. Pinion's *A Brontë Companion*, 377-82 (London: The Macmillan Press Ltd., 1975).

3 This tale has also been published by the Juvenilia Press, edited by Juliet McMaster and others.

4 Identified by Alexander as Captain Henry Hastings (*ECB* II.ii.288).

5 Note how images of the opulent East are used to reinforce the sense of foreignness in what is, ostensibly, an African tale. Both Orient and Africa are suitably exotic and equally available to the colonising imagination.

NOTE ON THE TEXT AND ACKNOWLEDGEMENTS

The original manuscript booklet of *My Angria and the Angrians,* once in the Law Collection, is now listed as untraced. The whole narrative, written in a minuscule hand, seems to have been contained in a mere $17\frac{1}{2}$ pages. In the absence of a manuscript as copy text, we have consulted the text of T.J. Wise and J.A. Symington in the Shakespeare Head Brontë, but we have used the splendidly informed edition of Christine Alexander, in *An Edition of the Early Writings of Charlotte Brontë* (1991), as our copy text. Besides conforming this text to our house style in the matter of double quotes rather than single, for the reader's guidance we have supplied chapter divisions and titles, along with some illuminated capitals in the manner of some nineteenth-century novels.

Our thanks are due to Christine Alexander, for her unstinting help and advice all along the way, and to the publishers Basil Blackwell, for permission to draw on the Shakespeare Head Brontë texts.

FAMILY TREES

The Wellesleys

- **Duke of Wellington**, King of Senegambia (Wellington's Land)
  = Lady Catherine Packenham
  - **Charles Wellesley** (youngest), narrator for Charlotte
  - **Arthur Adrian Wellesley** (eldest), Marquis of Douro, Duke of Zamorna
    = 1. Lady Helen Victorine Gordon
    = 2. Marian Hume, Duchess of Douro
    = 3. **Mary Henrietta Percy**, Duchess of Zamorna, Queen of Angria
    - (by 1.) Ernest Edward Fitzarthur Wellesley
    - (by 2.) Arthur Julius Wellesley
    - (by 3.) **Victor Francis Wellesley** (twin)
    - (by 3.) **Julius Warner Wellesley** (twin)
    - (by 3.) Arthur Wellesley
    - (by 3.) Maria Wellesley
- Richard, Marquis of Wellington
  = 1. Lady Wellesley
  = 2. Louisa Vernon
  - **Lady Julia**
    = Edward Sydney, Prince of York

The Percys

- Edward Percy, Sr.
  = Lady Helen Percy
  - Alexander Percy, Rogue, Duke of Northangerland
    = 1. Augusta di Segovia
    = 2. Maria Henrietta Wharton, Lady Percy
    = 3. Lady Zenobia Ellrington, daughter of Lord Henry Ellrington and Pauline Louisada
    - **Mary Henrietta Percy** (= Arthur Adrian Wellesley)
    - **Edward Percy**
      = **Lady Maria Sneachie**
    - Col. William Percy
    - Henry Percy

Characters who appear in *My Angria and the Angrians* appear in **boldface** type.

His powdered hair and sternly statuesque physiognomy at once announced the Duke of Wellington (36).

My Angria[1] and the Angrians,

By

Lord Charles Albert Florian Wellesley[2]

October 14 1834

[I. *In which the Angrians travel to the Promised Land.*]

The Children of Israel are gone up from amongst us,[3] and a mixed multitude went up with them, and flocks and herds and very much *cattle*. They went by the way of Baal-Zephon and are camped in the wilderness of *Sin*. (I believe the original orthography is Zin, but that signifies little.) A pillar of a cloud went before them, a pillar of a cloud by night and of fire by day (is not that the just description of King Adrian,[4] Angrians?) and in their departure they spoiled the Egyptians: they have not slain our first-born, but they have enticed them away, saying, cast in your lot with us and we will do you good. Hallelujah should now be the watchword throughout Verdopolis,[5] but alas, some there be who scruple not to cry "Ichabod, Ichabod, the glory is departed!"

With that love of ostentatious pomp and flashy display which circulates through the veins of every Angrian as unceasingly as his blood, the grand emigration was so contrived that at one day, almost at one hour, the carriage of each oriental noble[6] stood at the door of his Verdopolitan residence, and in splendid cortège the gathered host of vehicles with their attendant outriders went pouring from sunrise to sunset—a tide of thunder along the Eastern Highway. Previously had been the farewell visits and the last interviews, the solemn prognostications, the significant shakes of the head of the old régime, the insolent bantering and triumphant hilarity of the juvenile upstarts. I saw a certain fair and royal lip curled with so haughty and exulting an expression, as she bowed her head in parting salutation to one of her quondam friends, that it seemed as if the concentrated essence of refined (not vulgar) Angrianism had prompted the smile and the bright tantalizing glance that accompanied it.

It was hard for a steady sober Glass-Towner[7] (to say nothing of an irritable old aristocrat) to endure the swaggering effrontery of those latter days. To see the throngs of high-born scoundrels, the hordes of low-born rascallions, justling about from house to house and from street to street, talking loudly and incessantly of their preparations for the "Great Move," which preparations in the majority of cases must have been limited to the packing up of the second shirt, neckcloth and pair of stockings, together with the careful securing of the sow's ear containing the only half sovereign in shillings and pence,[8] which treasure must of necessity be placed in the adventurer's fob[9] unencumbered by watch, lest some of his travelling companions, in the ardour of their enterprising dispositions, might have proved their dexterity on his person, lightening him of the filthy lucre[10] while he sat unsuspiciously reposing himself on the ale bench of the Rising Sun or the Scarlet Banner or the Northangerland Arms.

To hear these fellows, I say, alluding with such a puppyish air of scorn to the old city where they dwelt so long, the home of their fathers, the Queen of the Earth, who looks down on her majestic face mirrored in the noble Niger[11] and sees the far reflection of her valley and her turrets caught by the flashing Guadiama[12] and flung with beauty unimaginable on the glass that her harbour gives her, to hear them prefer the marble toy shop of Adrianopolis,[13] the mushroom of the Calabar,[14] to a Babylon[15] so steadfastly founded, an oak whose roots have struck so deep as the city of the Guinea Coast, is most hateful, most maddening to any man cursed with a tithe less folly than themselves.

There, reader, you see how prettily I have worked myself up to a Sydneyan, a St Dairian or an Ardrahian passion![16] The fact is I care not a fig for the matter: the raff have a right to clear out for anything I know and if they chuse to shog[17] simultaneously why, let them. Verdopolis is well rid of their presence! Such, however, is unhappily not the opinion of all her inhabitants, as a proof whereof take the following extract from a three-sheet epistle addressed by the Honourable Julia, Lady Sydney,[18] to her bosom friend Lady Maria Percy.[19] After many professions of profound and immortal attachment, which the Crack of Doom[20] is neither to destroy nor interrupt, she continues:

"Oh Maria, how I envy you! Your destiny is, I think, nearly commensurate with your deserts! To be the very first goddess of the Angrian court (for I class you before Lady N—[21]), the wife of the handsomest and ablest Angrian minister, the daughter-in-law of the Great Angrian Premier,[22] the Arbitratress of the Angrian Modes, the Belle, the Toast, the Rose of the Angrian Beauties! Why, my dear, do you not sometimes feel giddy with your exalted elevation? I'm sure I should, my head would turn—but you, Maria, were born to grandeur, and the composed dignity with which you bear its honours shows they are your natural due. Meantime I fear I shall be utterly forgotten. Edward, I suppose, has filled up all the corners of your heart, and every lighter thought is devoted to *dear* Angria and the glories of its dazzling court. Pity me, Maria, if I am become too insignificant to love. Think of my situation—alone, alone in a wilderness of brick and marble. You cannot imagine how dark and dismal Verdopolis now seems to me. The sun, I believe, both rises and sets in the east—at any rate, its beams never find their way through the windows of York Place.[23]

"*My* Edward[24] grows more acid than ever. His features are getting so sourly contracted, that I fancy they will soon form an indistinguishable mass. Politics are to him food, drink, washing and lodging. He lives, moves and has his being[25] in their atmosphere; not a thought can he spare for anything else. We have no parties but political ones, no conversations but such as turn on affairs of state. Our uprising and our down-lying[26] are regulated by the length or brevity of a Cabinet council. His very dreams are suggested by the squabbles and disputes of the ministry. You would laugh till you cried to see how manfully he fights in his sleep, the arms and the features working up and down like those of a possessed person, and the tongue jabbering at intervals such words as 'My country! Ruinous schemes! Rotten administration! Unprincipled innovators!', etc.[27]

"This, however, is nothing new; it is all on the old tack. Home was always to me a dullish sort of place, except on gala nights, but now, alas, I am denied the privilege of finding matters somewhat brighter abroad. Yesterday evening, after spending the whole day in moping and fretting, I ordered the carriage and, as a dernier ressort,[28] drove to the Theatre Royal. While the people on the stage were performing their antics, I, instead of watching them, sat mourning over the altered aspect of the house. The dress tier of boxes seemed absolutely desolate. True, there were people in them and people, too, of loftiest rank and birth. Plenty of ancient countesses with their diamond bandeaux and nodding plumes.[29] Plenty of honourable misses not yet arrived at the centre of their teens; abundance of hoary earls, venerable viscounts, veteran general officers, etc., etc. But when I looked for Castlereagh, the noble, dashing dandy; for Arundel the gallant, courteous chevalier; for Edward Percy the haughty and handsome, who at intervals few and far between used formerly to appear like a star in his box under the chandelier; for Northangerland with his countenance of such strange and interesting melancholy; for honest Thornton[30] who always came to see the play and not to look about him; for Roslyn, for Seymour, for Abercorn, for Lennox; I protest, Maria, when I looked for all these and saw nothing but old Trojans[31] and their dowager dames, I had much ado to keep the tears from running down my cheeks. Then, as to the ladies, where, darling, were your own black eyes and long raven curls? Where were our Harrietta's graceful-looking though almost colourless features? Where was Lady Arundel's tall stately figure? Where was the imposing Countess Zenobia?[32] You remember how imperially she used to sit, her keen[33] gaze fixed on the stage and Lord N— placed beside her, attired in his mourning black with the earl's star gleaming on his bosom. (I always thought that dress peculiarly fascinating by the bye.) Where, too, was Mary Percy[34] (I never can somehow bring myself to call her by any other name), serene and proud, not often turning her head, and, when she did, regarding the person who had attracted her notice with that shyly piercing glance of hers which sometimes, when I have suddenly looked up and seen it fixed on me, has made the very flesh creep on my bones. Where were all these? Heigho! Just one hundred and fifty miles off. Maria, I'm very near heart-broken. You can't imagine how low-spirited and nervous I feel! Write to me soon, or I shall become a confirmed hypochondriac. Your letters are the only consolation now left me. If that fails, I really see nothing for it but felo de se."[35]

So much for Lady Julia, poor thing! The departure of the Angrians has put her in a cruel taking. What's to be done? She'd better sue for a separate maintenance.[36] Leave Sydney to his bride, the state, and at once take wing for some fashionable bower in her adored Eastern Paradise.[37]

[II *In which Lord Charles Wellesley meets with a traveller in the Park Road.*]

Reader,[38] how differently are the minds of mortals constituted! The very same privilege which Julia Sydney pines and weeps after, Charles Wellesley[39] spurns and contemns. Previously to General Thornton's departure for Adrianopolis, he did everything in his power to induce me to accompany him. In vain were promises, threats, even blows. I grinned at him; I mocked him; I scratched him and I rebelled against [him]! Was I going to enlist voluntarily as a subject of the despot? No! I stood firm and Wilkin was forced to leave Girnington Hall[40] without me. Five weary days did I reign Lord Paramount in the panelled dens of that hoary mansion, and at length, sick of seclusion, I reflected that it would perhaps be as well to amuse myself by going up and spying out the nakedness of the land,[41] not that the act of doing so would not infer subjection to Thornton. On the evening of the sixth day[42] I formed this resolution and determined to put it in practice on the morrow. Accordingly, before the sun had risen, next morning I was up, dressed and walking alone down the Park Road. Yes, reader, I who might have commanded a carriage and a posse of attendants, chose to set out on a journey of one hundred miles with no aid but such as my own bodily limbs afforded me, and the perspective chance of a cast[43] in the carts or waggons I might meet on my way.

Girnington Park is almost a wood, for, being of old date, the trees have gradually thickened and heightened, till such slips of pasture as remain between their overgrown trunks and huge branches present the aspect of forest glades. They were lingering in twilight as I passed through them. Here and there a silvan roe might be discerned gliding behind some Goliath-like oak, or slender pale-barked birch, and at intervals a flushed pheasant whirred from his perch, or a wakening stock-dove cooed low and deep from his still nest in the farthest recesses of the wood, but every other sound at that hour was not.

By means of a pass key, which I carry unknown to Thornton, the massy gates which shut in these grounds unfolded to my touch. I closed and locked them after me and thus freed from the Castle of Giant Despair,[44] went on my way rejoicing. Cool and balmy sighed the sunrise breeze over all that green prospect that lay in dew before, behind and on each side of me. When I looked round, Edwardston Hall[45] and its village, nestling (as it seemed at this distance) on the very confines of the park, were putting off their veil of thin blue mist and lifting their roofs distinctly against the sky, as if inviting the first ray to gleam on them.

The horizon above Sydenham Hills[46] shone in that peculiar gold radiance, deepening to vivid crimson and then dying off to silver blue, which an autumnal morning can alone offer in perfection. The dawn of summer days is soft and bright but not so vividly tinted along the horizon as that which lights up the fall of the year. I glanced down the broad road, east and west: it was solitary, speckless; not so much as a bird hopped on its wide, white surface—white now, but fast yellowing to the kindled heaven.[47]

Being in no hurry, I threw myself under the hedge and sat to watch for a fellow traveller. Ere long something dark appeared gliding under the distant woods of Edwardston, so far off that at first its motion was scarcely perceptible. It drew nigh and nigher; the outline of a human figure became distinct. Still no sound was heard. A turn in the road hid it; it emerged again, only about eighty yards off, and, striding fast and firm, there advanced a low, slightly built man attired in a black coat and raven grey trowsers, his hat placed nearly at the back of his head, revealing a bush of carroty hair so arranged that at the sides it projected almost like two spread hands, a pair of spectacles placed across a prominent Roman nose, black neckerchief adjusted with no great attention to precision, and, to complete the picture, a little black ratan[48] flourished in the hand. His bearing as he walked was tolerably upright and marked with that indescribable swing always assumed by those who pride themselves on being good pedestrians. I rose at his approach and proceeded to accost him. "Well, Wiggins,"[49] said I (for it was no other), "How d'ye do? It's a fine morning."

"An uncommonly fine morning, Lord Charles. I'm excessively glad to see you. Hope you're going a good way along the road. Shall be proud of your company. That is, if you can keep up with me."

By means of a pass key, which I carry unknown to Thornton, the massy gates which shut in these grounds unfolded to my touch.

"O never fear, Wiggins, I'll do my best. But pray, are you going to the end of the world? I should think so from the spirit with which you progress."

"Not *quite* to the end of the world—that is, not altogether. Just at present, I don't think of walking much farther than Zamorna.[50] I came to Edwardston last night, and slept there. Mr. Greenwood[51] sent for me from Verdopolis. The distance, you know, Lord Charles, is forty miles and I did it all in twelve hours—indeed, it's more than forty, nearer fifty, I believe. O yes, and above sixty I daresay, or sixty-five.

Now sir, what do you see to a man's walking sixty-five miles in one day?' As I knew Wiggins's style of exaggeration I made no answer but by a nod, and he proceeded, 'They say there's going to be a grand do at Zamorna today, a county meeting about that adress to the Angrians. And Lord Castlereagh is to take the chair, and Mr Edward Percy is expected to be the principal speaker. I should so like to hear him! He walked one hundred miles in a day and night! A great man, a very great man! Wears just the right swallow-tailed sort of coat, with a high collar almost up to the curled crown of his head. I kneeled down at the gates of Edwardston Hall for half an hour and more this morning. Look at the knees of my trowsers! That clay, Lord Charles, has, I have no doubt, often been trodden upon by his feet. I wish my back could boast of the same honour, but it's exceedingly presumptuous of me to say so. He would scorn such footing!"

Just then the tramp of a horse behind us interrupted Wiggins's oratory. We turned. Riding at a rapid trot, on a splendid bay horse, appeared the identical subject of my companion's panegyric. He was alone, and he little needed servants to increase his air of rank and consequence. Seated so proudly upright in the saddle, the reins grasped with firm grace and masterly skill, all his equipments in such perfect order, burnished spurs, and stirups glittering like gold, bit and bridle displaying the polish of pure silver, boots black as jet, the olive-brown coat and cream coulour pantaloons, cut evidently by a first-rate snip[52] and displaying the fine muscular symetry of the young athlete they enveloped to admirable advantage. His hawk-eyes were fixed straight forward and lighted his noble features like gems. They are blue in coulour but so fierily expressive I, for one, would not come under their glance when the torch of anger kindles them. He passed us without vouchsafing either word or look. I watched till distance concealed him, and then again turned to Wiggins. Lo, he was fallen upon his face flat as a fluke, motionless as a dead herring, prostrated towards the east like a Parsee[53] worshipping the new risen sun.

"Benjamin," said I, "get up! What's the use of playing the fool when there's only me to see you."

He made no answer and I know not how long he would have continued in the same position, had not a sound like distant thunder announced the Angrian coach, and on it came, laden heavily within and without, the roof piled with packages, the horses smoking, the passengers joking, laughing and shouting, the guard and coachman swearing responsively. The rush and rattle were deafening as it swept by. They made Wiggins spring up pretty actively, but no sooner was he on his feet than he broke out with, "Base dung-hill cock that I am! Superannuated, doting blindworm, deformed mongrel, turnspit, wretch, thief, highwayman, assassin, murderer, pickpocket, petty larcenist, dog-stealer, essence of plague, pestilence and famine! What *am* I that I should live after having seen Percy, the son of Northangerland, pass by, and without either shooting or spitting at me! Why didn't I throw myself under the wheels of that coach, like a Hindoo beneath the car of Juggernaut?[54] And I daresay there were great men contained in it too! I thought I heard a bass voice speaking like Wolverton Talbot, Rogue's champion. Did you ever see him, Lord Charles? He's a dark, broad, beetle-browed man, as tough as if he was all made out of Indian-rubber. And he swears in such a glorious way! He's been a pirate, and wouldn't care for killing a man just now any more than he would for eating an onion. But, dear me, what am I saying? How can I think, talk or dream about anybody except Mr. Edward Percy, riding along on that grand horse which must be worth five hundred guineas—that is, eight hundred, or else a thousand—at such an early hour, and without either footman or page or any such trash trailing after him? He's determined to reach Zamorna first and order all things according to his own will. I hope he'll command abundance of accommodation to be provided for the bands of music, or else Mr. Greenwood'll not be pleased, no more will Mr. Rohner, nor Mr. Nicholson, nor Dr. Crotch. By a by, Lord Charles, there are to be five brass bands, each consisting of two trumpets, three bombardones, four cyclopedes, five serpents, six bugles, seven French horns, eight gongs, nine kettle drums, and ten ramgalongtonas,[55] a new kind of instrument that's never been blown in Africa before. And then the five wood-bands will contain eleven flutes (all by Nicholson), twelve clarinets, thirteen piccolos —"

"Spare us, Wiggins," interrupted I. "Why, man, according to your calculation of musical instruments the courthouse will be entirely taken up by them and their manager. However, put this Zamorna business out of your head a short time, if you can, and answer a few questions I shall ask you respecting your own particular self. In the first place, where did you first see the light? What part of Africa had the honour of giving you birth?"

"Why, Lord, Charles, I was born partly at Thorncliffe, that is, after a fashion, but then I always account myself a native of Howard,[56] a great city among the Warner Hills, under the dominion of that wonderful and superhuman gentleman Warner Howard Warner,[57] Esqr" (here he took off his hat and bowed low). "It has four churches and above twenty grand hotels, and a street called the Taan Gate, far wider than Bridgenorth in Free Town."[58]

"None of your humbug, Wiggins!" said I. "I know well enough Howard is only a miserable little village, buried in dreary moors and moss-hags[59] and marshes. I question whether it has one church or anything nearer an hotel than that wayside ale-house you are now eyeing so longingly."

"I'm rather thirsty," replied he. "And I think I'll call for a pot of porter or a tumbler of brandy and water, at the public yonder." He bolted across the road.

A fat landlady met him at the door. "Well, sir, what's your will?" said she, for he stood a moment without speaking.

"If you please, ma'am, will you be kind enough to give me a ha'-penny'orth of milk, or a gill of whey, or even a draught of ditch water, if it would be too much trouble to procure the other liquids for such a mere tom-cat as I am."

The hostess, who seemed to be a good-natured soul, was no doubt accustomed to Wiggins's manner, as he is a frequent traveller on this road. She laughed and said: "You'd better step into the house, sir, and get a cup of warm tea into you. I've set the breakfast things on the table."

Wiggins scraped his feet very carefully and followed her in. I could see him, through the open door, take a seat by the fireside, swallow two or three cups of tea, with a due quantum of bread and butter very rapidly dismissed. Then, rising from his seat, he took from his pocket about twenty shillings in silver (how he came by it I don't know) and offering it with an air to the landlady said, "Pay yourself out of that, ma'am, just take what you will, I never call a reckoning." She helped herself, laughing at the same time, and with a gallant "good morning," he quitted the house and rejoined me.

"Well!" was his first exclamation. "I feel like a lion now, at any rate. Two bottles of Sneachie's Glass-Town[60] ale, and a double quart of porter, with cheese, bread and cold beef have I devoured since I left you, Lord Charles. That's what I call doing the thing in a handsome way! And I'm not a bit touched—only light and smart and active. I'd defy all the ganders in Christendom now, that I would, and a hundred goslings to boot! But, however, let us re-piece-en[61] the talk. What were you asking me, sir?"

"I asked you where you were born, sir, and now I ask you what relations you have?"

"Why, in a way, I may be said to have no relations. I can't tell who my father and mother were no more than that stone. I've some people who call themselves akin to me in the shape of three girls. They are honoured by possessing me as a brother, but I deny that they're my sisters. Robert Patrick Sdeath, Esqr. is partly my uncle, but he's the only relative I'll acknowledge."

"What are your sisters' names?"

"Charlotte Wiggins, Jane Wiggins and Anne Wiggins."[62]

"Are they as queer as you?"

I could see him, through the open door, take a seat by the fireside, swallow two or three cups of tea, with a due quantum of bread and butter

"Oh, they are miserable silly creatures not worth talking about. Charlotte's eighteen years old, a broad dumpy thing, whose head does not come higher than my elbow. Emily's sixteen, lean and scant, with a face about the size of a penny, and Anne is nothing, absolutely nothing."

"What! Is she an idiot?"

"Next door to it."

"Humph, you're a pretty set! But pray, Master Wiggins, what first induced you [to] leave Howard and come to Verdopolis?"

"Why you see, Lord Charles, my mind was always looking above my station. I wasn't satisfied with being a sign-painter at Howard, as Charlotte and them things were with being sempstresses.[63] I set before myself the Grand Plain of Africa, and I traced a path for my own feet through it, which terminated at the door of a splendid palace situate on Cock Hill, whose portal bore inscribed 'Residence of the Duke of Thorncliffe', and beyond that a tomb under the oaks of my own park, showing to the passenger such words as these 'Erected to the memory [of] Patrick Benjamin Wiggins, Duke of Thorncliffe and Viscount Howard. As a musician he was greater than Bach; as a poet he surpassed Byron; as a painter, Claude Lorrain yielded to him; as a rebel he snatched the palm from Alexander Rogue; as a merchant Edward Percy was his inferior; as a mill-owner Grenville came not near him; as a traveller De Humbolt, Ledyard, Mungo Park,[64] etc., etc., never braved half his dangers or overcame half his difficulties. He civilized Australia; he founded the city of Wigginopolis in New Zealand. He erected the obelisk of Baraliticus in Otaheite,[65] to which country he also introduced the arts and sciences which now flourish there in such perfection, and the last and greatest of his mighty acts, he built the stupendous organ called Rollrogthunder-asqueakbotherboreimus now glorifying the Cathedral of St Northangerland in his native place of Howard. Having earned all this meed of renown and attained his four hundred and sixth year, this summum bonus of human grandeur was at length rapt to heaven in a fiery chariot,[66] which miraculous event took place about the year two thousand two hundred and forty.'

"With ideas so sublime as these in my mind, you may imagine, Lord Charles, how I longed for an extended field to put them into practice. At length, the wished-for opportunity arrived. In the month of May last a fine and full new horgan was hoppened in Howard Church. At that period, John Greenwood, Esqr, the musician and composer, chanced to return from his sojourn in Stumpsland,[67] being wholly destitute of the means of existence, and so forlorn that he had neither penny in his pocket, shoes on his feet or a shirt to his back. That great man was compelled, shortly after landing, to seek a temporary refuge in the house of a humble acquaintance of his, one Mr Sudbury Figgs, who resided within four miles of Howard, and who, being a pianist by profession, was accustomed to give music lessons to the various families in the neighbourhood. When I heard of his arrival, I stood upon my head for fifteen minutes running! It was news almost too glorious to be believed! But afterwards, when Mr Abey Figgs[68] told me, as he was drinking tea at our house, that through his influence Mr Greenwood had been prevailed on to preside at the horgan's hoppening and re-hoppening (for the business was twice performed) I positively fell into a fit with joy. He came—I saw him—yes, I remember the moment when he entered the church, walked up to the organ gallery where I was, kicked Sudbury Figgs, who happened to be performing Handel's 'And the Glory of the Lord,' from the stool, and assuming it himself, placed his fingers on the keys, his feet on the pedals, and proceeded to electrify us with 'I Know that My Redeemer Liveth.'[69]

"'Then,' said I, 'this is a god and not a man!'[70] As long as the music sounded in my ears, I dared neither speak, breathe, nor even look up. When it ceased, I glanced furtively at the performer. My heart had previously been ravished by the mere knowledge of his fame and skill, but not resistlessly was it captivated, when I saw in Mr Greenwood a tall man dressed in black, with a pair of shoulders, light complexion and hair inclining to red—my very beau ideal of personal beauty, carrying even some slight and dim resemblance to the notion I had formed of Rogue. Instantly I assumed that inverted position which with me is alway a mark of highest astonishment, delight and admiration. In other words I clapt my pate to the ground and let my heels fly up with a spring. They happened to hit Mr Sudbury Figgs's chin, as he stood in his usual way, picking his teeth and projecting his under jaw a yard beyond the rest of his countenance. He exclaimed so loud as to attract Mr Greenwood's attention. He turned round and saw me. 'What's that fellow playing his mountebank tricks here for?' I heard him say. Before anybody could answer I was at his feet licking the dust under them[71] and crying aloud, 'O Greenwood! The greatest, the mightiest, the most famous of men! Doubtless you are ignorant of a nit, the goal of a louse, like me, but I have learnt to know you through the medium of your wonderful works. Suffer the basest of creatures to devote himself utterly to your service, as a shoe-black, a rosiner of fiddlesticks, a greatcoat-carrier, a port-music, in short as a thorough-going toadie.'

"Greenwood laughed. He gave me permission to stand by his side. That night I handed him his hat when he left the church, tumbling over William Rad, Henry Lock and John Mildmay (the organ-builder's son) in my hurry to get it. Afterwards I had the supreme felicity of running down to the inn with his Indian neckerchief which he had left behind him. During the remainder of his stay at Howard I had various other little opportunities of currying favour with him. At last, one evening when he was sitting in the Black Bull[72] public house, together with Tom and John Rad, uncle and father to Billy Rad, and had just emptied his thirteenth tumbler of brandy and water, he told me that I might accompany him to Verdopolis when he went there and welcome. Before my extacy of thanksgiving and gratitude was over, he rose and told me to pack up my alls, for he was going to set off that minute for the crossroads, where a coach passed westward at ten o'clock p.m. I just ran home to tell the children, got my best clothes, my clean shirt and collar, and in an hour's time was rattling as fast as four coach-horses could carry me towards Free Town. I saw the next day's sun set behind the Tower of All Nations! And so, Lord Charles, there's the history of my emigration from Howard to Verdopolis."

* * * * * * * * * * * * * * *

[III. *In which Lord Charles enters the great metropolis of Zamorna and meets with beauty upon an occasion of public importance.*]

Shortly after Wiggins had concluded his strange narration, which shewed an odd mixture of folly and enterprise, absurd toadyism and bold ambition, we both entered the crowded streets of Zamorna. Just opposite the New Exchange we parted. He proceeded to find out Greenwood's residence, for that musical ignis-fatuus[73] has at present fixed his sojourn in this city, and I, "as aimless as the clouds that float a summer heaven upon,"[74] went wandering whither the spirit should lead me.

I think it was about noon when I reached the splendid suspension bridge which has lately been thrown over the Olympia. Here so thick was the throng of eager multitudes hurrying by the nearest way to the County Field, that, experienced as I am in working my way through crowds, I positively could get no farther. After one or two narrow escapes from being knocked down amongst the thundering carriages, rampant horses and innumerable pedestrians, I ran up the steps of one of the Tall Towers, and there stood as safe as the kid on the top of its shed. It was an animating scene that met my eyes from thence.

Immediately before me the numbers without number, numberless, streaming, trampling, rushing and rattling along, and in a long line blackening the wide breadth of Stuartville Road as it stretched downward to the place of rendezvous. Underneath, the rapid river, bright and blue and sparkling in sunlight, and in the reflection of a glorious autumn sky, all its swift life-like waves leaping as if they partook the triumph of the day but their voices now inaudible, for the noise of the mighty throng passing above them drowned every fainter sound. Eastward lay the

city, resounding with the ring of bells and the shouts of exultation echoing in every street. Edward Percy's New Mill[75] with its colossal chimney towered nobly from the sloping banks of the Olympia,[76] and the cottages and combing shops of his workmen clustered about it like pigmies guarding a giant. Opposite lay the County Field with the City Hall at the top and the hustings erected before it, which at this distance looked with its flags and awnings like a patch of scarlet decorating the front of that huge municipal edifice. The bands of music were already on the spot, and their swelling strains rose at intervals over the rejoicing storm that roared above them. Then there was the noble champaign of field and park and woodland stretching round the aerial girdle of the Zamorna Hills[77] and the farther heights of Sydenham, with heaven's own zone, the glowing noontide horizon bounding all.

While I stood gazing at this prospect, a carriage attended by outriders, etc., blazing in red and gold liveries, came dashing over the bridge. At a signal from the inmate it drew up before my stance. The door was dashed open. A voice said, "Bring him hither this minute!" And ere I was aware, I found myself hustled down the toll bar steps and crammed per force into the vehicle. A lady and two gentlemen occupied it. The former was my cousin Julia; the two latter were Mr Babicombe Morley and General Thornton. The first glimpse I obtained of this last mentioned assured me he was in an irate mood. The puckered eyebrows and ruddied forehead were indications sufficiently intelligible.

"Little villanous imp!"[78] was his first salutation. "What's brought thee to Zamorna on such a day as this, I wonder. When I wanted thee to follow me thou wert pig-headed to stay at Girnington and now, when I shall have more nor enow to do to mind myself among this raff o'horses and folks and carriages, here I find thee stuck like a monkey on the brig-stairs. If I live, thou'st be sorted this night afore thy head touches a pillow!"

"Nay, General," said Lady Sydney, "don't let the little whelp disturb you so. I'll take him under my protection. Charles, will you go with me to the ladies' seats?"

"That's as thereafter may be," replied I. "But pray, Julia, how did you come here? Whose visitor are you?"

"Lady Maria's. She sent me such a kind and pressing invitation, and I told Sydney I *would* accept it. He said I should *not*, but for once I was determined to be master, so when he left the house, I took French leave, called my maid and the chariot, and hey for Angria!"

And now we reached the very thick of the commotion. Our foaming steeds bore us into the County Field and as we entered it at one inlet Lord Castlereagh, Mr Percy, Lord Arundel, Colonel Hartford,

While I stood gazing at this prospect, a carriage attended by outriders, etc., blazing in red and gold liveries, came dashing over the bridge.

Lord Dance, etc., etc., were thundering in at the other. The bands broke out with Marseilles's inspiring glee "Welcome Heroes to the War."[79] The embodied voice of all that multitude rolled in a peal of applauding thunder from the river to the suburbs of Zamorna. We dashed on and on up to the hustings. We alighted. Thornton and Morley joined the other gentlemen, and I and Julia ascended the stage which had been erected for the accommodation of the principal ladies. With what a stately air did she glide along to her station by Maria Percy, who, with the Lady Lieutenant and the Countess of Arundel,[80] occupied the centre of the front seat.

When the four were seated I looked at them. It was a splendid sight. Maria shone fairest of the fair, flushed as she was with excitement, sparkling with triumph. I never beheld a brighter vision. Her robes were all of scarlet, and her radiantly white neck, her jetty hair and eyes exquisitely relieved that dazzling dress. The three other ladies wore scarlet scarves and plumes, but the rest of their attire was white satin. They too were lovely, graceful, fascinating, and by a strange coincidence all happened to be dark complexioned. Edith, Julia, Harriet, every one black-tressed brunettes. By the bye, some people say Lady Arundel is not a thorough-going Angrian. I beg to correct this mistake. She speaks little about it, but her own Frederick bows not down in more devoted worship of the Rising Sun than she does. When she gave her heart to the chivalric Arundel, she gave it not by halves but undivided. His "gods became her gods and his country her country."[81] This day I saw her put her hair from her noble brow and gaze with a piercing look of almost wild enthusiasm on the living ocean which roared and thundered around her on the hustings, with its background of the gloomy and stupendous hall, its gilded banners red as blood, so brilliantly vermilion in the lights, so gory in the shadows, and its vigorous, stately occupants, each as kindled and as earnest then as if a nation's fate depended on the hour just passing. Thence her eye wandered to the open country, the sunlit town, the broad Olympia, its banks here piled with buildings and there spread with tree-dropped and cattle-specked pasture.

"Maria," said she, turning to her sister, "we have Highland blood in our veins; we are the daughters of a monarch; but subjects in this glorious land, wedded to two beings so glorious as thy Edward and my Frederick. See, they are now standing together. We need not remember sadly the Palace of St Mary, the hill of Elimbos, the loch[82] of the Genii[83] or even our brother Fidena." Maria smiled triumphantly and clasped Lady Arundel's hand, but she said nothing.

Meantime I observed Lady Julia's sparkling merry glance was directed to other things than the sublimity of the scene. She had spied out Mr Charles Warner and Mr John Howard at a short distance in the crowd and was now beckoning them to approach. Her ivory fan and her as ivory arm were raised with an arch, graceful gesture, and the scarlet plumes nodded proudly on her head as she bent it coquettishly to one side. They came as fast [as] they could push through intervening obstacles. With charming frankness, half-assumed and half-real, Julia held out both her hands, giving one to each.

"My dear Mr Charles, my dear Mr John, I'm delighted to see you! Quite an unexpected pleasure! I feared Mr Warner would require your presence at Angria[84] in these busy times, and it would have been such a disappointment." For a minute neither of the gentlemen answered, but each stood vigorously thrusting his elbow into the other's side as a hint that he should speak first. At last Charles replied. "My lady," said he, "we're vastly obliged to ye. You've a very fine turn of

"My dear Mr Charles, my dear Mr John, I'm delighted to see you!"

compliment indeed. Pity 'at John here doesn't deserve much civility being thrown away on him."

"Nay now, Charles," grumbled John, "that's not what I call drawing it mild![85] The lady was as polite to me as you and thinks as much of me."

"Indeed I do!" returned Julia. "You're such a pair as the world will never behold again. But, gentlemen, why are you not on the hustings? Of course you intend to speak."

Both looked down with a modest blush. "Why, madam," said Charles, "John here never was given to speak much. He hasn't a turn that way, as we may say. I'm better in gifts, but since my late misfortune I've declined appearing often in public. People take occasion to joke you know, madam, and that's what I don't like."

"Your late misfortune, my dear sir? I never heard of it, surely nothing serious —"

"Serious, my lady! Aye, but it is! Look ye here," and he held up his right hand, mutilated of the little finger. Julia repressed a laugh with great difficulty. "Well, Mr Charles," she went on in a consoling tone, "'Tis a sad thing certainly, a derogation from your once perfect manhood, as one may say, but still I don't see how that should hinder you from speaking, and I must insist that both you and Mr John condescend to enlighten this meeting by your wisdom. Now do, gentleman, just to please me." She leaned over the stage and looked down on the squires with a most sweetly supplicating smile, and Charles was melted.

"John," said he, administering an energetic dig to his brother worthy's ribs. "What do you say, it wouldn't be polite to refuse her ladyship, and our head didn't forbid us speaking. He only said he hoped we shouldn't be such fools as to attempt to speak."

"Very true, Charles, so come along. We'll astonish him by making a speech as long and broad as one of his own!"

They bowed to Julia and, moving away, were soon lost among the multitude. And now the business of the day commenced. Amidst deafening cheers Mr Edward Percy advanced to the front of the hustings. He stood silent till they subsided, and, in that interval, never saw I such exulting fire as flashed from his lighted eyes. Of his speech I shall only say that it was worthy

Of his speech I shall only say that it was worthy of him, full of energy…

of him, full of energy, of close and cogent argument, occasionally tinctured with an air of swagger, especially when he alluded to the great Northangerland, but on the whole it might be called an Angrian oration of the highest order, and so the listeners felt it. Tremendous was the burst of applause that greeted him as he resumed his seat. As it subsided, other speakers advanced. All with more or less ability spoke in the same strain and were cheered with enthusiasm proportionate to their merits. At last, towards the close of the day, when the people were getting obstreperously loud, joyous and tumultuous, Castlereagh called from the chair Mr Charles Warner. That personage stepped blushing forth, closely and fraternally backed by his loving cousin John. Amid the boisterous roar of the meeting, his voice could only be heard at intervals. What follows is a literal transcript of this most eloquent effusion:

"Gentlemen" (cheers) "you are very kind but" (loud cheers) "owing to a late calamitous accident" (continued cheering) "which involved the loss of a precious limb" (here the right honourable gentleman found himself unable to proceed from emotion; recovering, however, he went on), "Angrians, if it had not been for the pressing entreaties of a lady" (tremendous applause) "the fairest of her sex. I say, John, don't you think she's very handsome?"

(John in sotto-voce, twirling his beaver, smoothing it and looking modestly down) "Aye, she'd like as what we mud call a personabilish sort of a woman." (Cheers which lasted several minutes.)

Mr Charles, in continuation: "I ventured to intrude a few words on your notice" (yells, shouts and cheering mixed). "Our head—that's John's and mine—objects to a deal of talk" (cheers),—"so I'll compress" (renewed cheers) "in a few words" (a perfect earthquake of applause). "Gentlemen, this is the proudest day of my life—I—I—I feel quite overcome" (shouts of huzza, and go on, hear him, etc.). "I've not much time to spare. Didn't Warner tell us to be back by six o'clock, John?"

"Aye, Charles, and it's half after five already."

"Gentlemen, I beg leave to second the resolution and having expressed my—my—my" (thunders of applause), "I'll sit down."

Mr C. Warner resumed his seat amidst such a roar of mingled sounds, laughter, bravos, howling, etc., etc., that it was found impossible to make any other speaker heard. The noble chairman therefore called for a round of nine times nine for Zamorna and Angria, and this over, proclaimed the meeting dissolved. Instantly the bands again lifted their storm-like harmony. Bugles rung, drums thundered, trumpets swelled exultingly, the crowd swayed to and fro in grand commotion, the huge and thronging banners heavily hung above them, all their folds waving to the slow breeze and the plunging motions of their bearers.

At this moment a gentleman of tall and powerful figure dashed through the multitude and at one bound cleared the paling erected before the hustings, mounted them very unceremoniously and, stretching out his arms as he stood erect in the front, said in a clear, trumpet-like voice that rose over and almost quelled the din, "Men of Angria, before one among you strides a step homeward, let all join in our grand national anthem. 'Sound the loud trumpets o'er Afric's dark sea'. Bands, strike into the air!"[86]

Stranger though the speaker was, he found prompt obedience. His commanding manner, the startling depth and grandeur of his tone, and the nature of his proposal, all found favour in the sight of those who heard him, and soon up burst that sublime song with a sound so loud, so full, so deep in its cadences, so triumphant in its swells, that it seemed as if the thunders sung in heaven, and the winds and seas of earth made answer to them. It died rolling, echoing along the arrowy river, spending its last notes at the foot of Sydenham's long moorland range. Now there was a pause of silence.

"Well done," continued the stranger, "that had some heart. Thank ye, my lads, for your compliance."

He jumped from his station and, keeping still within the paling, came slowly walking along towards the ladies' seats. Of course, they all looked at him, and I thought many a bright eye lingered on his form[87] and followed it anxiously as he passed. He regarded them, too, with a careless and condescending smile which brightened into flashing pride as his glance turned on the now departing multitude. He paused just opposite to where I sat and thus I was enabled to take a full and leisurely view of him. He seemed to be in the full bloom of youth: his figure was toweringly, overbearingly lofty, moulded in statue-like perfection, and invested with something which I cannot describe—something superb, impetuous, resistless, something, in short, no single word can altogether express. His hair was intensely black, curled luxuriantly, but the forehead underneath, instead of having the swarthy tinge proper to such Italian locks, looked white and smooth as ivory. His eyebrows were black and broad, but his long eyelashes and large clear eyes were deep sepia brown. The wreaths on his temples were brought so low as to meet the profusely curled raven whiskers and mustachios which hid his mouth and chin and shadowed his fair complexioned cheeks. I thought these symbols of manhood much too strong and abundant for his evident juvenility. When he smiled, lips and teeth appeared such as any lady might have envied, coral-red and pearl-white. The upper lip was very short, Grecian, and had a haughty curl which I knew well. At the first glance I discerned him to be a military man. The erect bearing, composed martial nonchalance, and measured stately stride told that plainly enough. Even his dress, though undistinguished by lace, plume, sword-belt or epaulette, was entirely of the soldier cast: blue coat, black stock, white vest and pantaloons, fur foraging cap, placed forward so that the rim sternly darkened his brow and brilliant eyes, boots of the highest polish, made with the exact tightness best calculated to display the perfect symmetry of his small Circassian[88] foot.

"That's a proper man!" said Maria Percy when she had carefully surveyed him. "One of the few I should condescend to look twice at. Pray, does anyone here know him? Ask my sister-in-law Cecillia there, and Lady Richton. They are whispering intelligently."

"Did Maria mention my name?" asked the mild, arch Cecillia Percy, bending forward.

"Yes, girl, I wish to know if you are acquainted with that black-headed Titan?"

"No," she replied drily. "Are you, Matilda?" (to Lady Richton). "No," was the brief response. "On my honour I'll ask his name," continued Maria.

"Surely you will not," interposed Edith coldly. "He cannot be anyone of much consequence."

"I will, though. And that too in a manner which shall not make him proud of the notice."

"Do, do," said Lady Sydney, "You always go to the root of the matter at once, Maria."

In all the pride of her rank and beauty the Princess bent over the stage. "Come hither, sir," said she imperiously. He turned his head but not his person.

"Well, pretty one, what do you want?" was the astounding familiar adress to one of the proudest and fairest women of Africa. This would have done my cousin Julia up; it only spirited Maria to go forward.

"What do I want, sir? Nothing more than your name, that I may report you to the proper authorities for having intruded within the paling."

"Good," said the stranger. "You desire me to bear testimony against myself! Not so, Sparkler."

"I will have you arrested on the spot, if you do not obey me. My servants are at hand," continued the roused and angry Princess.

"Wilt thou?" said the stranger in a lowered and changed tone. Maria started, blushed over neck, brow and temples, and sunk back in her seat as quiet as a lamb. He laughingly advanced towards her. "Come, madam," said he, "I had no intention to quarrel with one

"Do, do," said Lady Sydney, "You always go to the root of the matter at once, Maria."

who is so perfectly unknown to me as yourself. My name is Major Albert Howard, formerly of Wastwater Forest in the west, but now of Mournely Crag in Arundel. I was not aware that any restriction existed regarding this paling, so you must forgive my intrusion."

"I do," said Maria, bowing and smiling very graciously. Major Albert smiled too, but his haughty head refused to bend, and in silence he moved slowly away.

"How could I be so obtuse?" murmured Maria when he was gone. Cecillia's fair face again leaned over her shoulder.

"*Him* for a wager, sister," she said archly.

"Or else his wraith," returned the Princess.

"What, with black hair like your own, Mary?"

"Yes, or even had it been golden like thine, Cicely."

"The less said about it the better," remarked Lady Arundel.

"I don't know what you're all whispering so mysteriously about," said Lady Julia. "The man is very handsome and I am sure a gentleman. He reminds me of my cousin Zamorna more than any living creature I ever saw before. Why, bless me, do you think it can be him in disguise—dyed hair, false whiskers, changed dress, assumed voice? It is! It is! Oh, I wish I had spoken to him! And Maria, that was what made you blush so! The tone of that 'Wilt thou?' was utterly Zamornaic! But then—Major Howard, Wastwater Forest! Mournely

Crag. No, no, I fear it can't be! And the whiskers didn't look artificial, did they Harriet?"

"Why," said Lady Castlereagh, "if such whiskers sprung from such a skin there's no faith in complexion,[89] that's all."

The gentlemen of the hustings now began to approach. Castlereagh dashed up in high glee. "Well, my Lady Sydney, you here! Delightful! What d'ye think of the meeting? Gone off like a shot, hasn't it? Unanimous feeling, proper manifestation of spirit, highly pleased. His Majesty ought to be satisfied with the adress. Did I make a good chairman? Did I give satisfaction?"

"In this quarter, the most complete satisfaction, my lord."

"In this quarter! The only one worth caring for! Obliged to you for the compliment! Ha, ha, ha! Very good! Surena, my pocket handkerchief." Surena immediately produced a square of scarlet silk nearly large enough to form the mainsail of a man of war. His lordship flourished and fluttered it about some five or six minutes, spreading its scents of eau-de-Cologne, poudre des œillets, otto des roses, etc., etc., all round, then blew his aristocratic nose, projected his as aristocratic saliva some twenty yards and continued. "A deal of oratory. Part of it considerably decent stuff, too. Edward Percy's turned out not bad, my own likewise, though I say it, very tolerable, and Morley there, if it hadn't been for his infernal boreishness about intellect and useless knowledge and entertaining humbug."

"Order, my Lord Castlereagh, order!" exclaimed Morley who stood near. "I call your lordship to order. You act with malice prepense in naming those three substantives so contemptuously to the lady. Now, madam, if you will give me leave to lucubrate for thirty consecutive minutes in your presence, I will undertake to prove in a manner which shall give you the most pleasing mental consolation and which shall now and for ever shut out all doubts on the subject, that intellect, knowledge and humbug are the three condiments which keep society sweet. Your ladyship is aware there are thirteen ways of taking a distinction, five real and eight assumed for the sake of argument. Now to these thirteen I shall add a fourteenth in order to make the number equal and proceed forwith to divide my discourse into its several heads. Firstly then —"

"Save me!" interrupted Julia. "For heaven's sake, Mr Morley, shew a little forbearance. I'll hear you some other time, in private, more at my ease, but now —"

"But now your ladyship shall hear *me*," said the heavy voice of Charles Warner, and he and John rushed like giants refreshed with wine. They at once seized Julia's unresisting hands. "My dear, excellent lady." almost sobbed Charles, "you're like a jewel of gold in a swine's snout if ever a woman was. If it hadn't been for you I should never have known what was in me and so it couldn't have come out as it has done today."

"Didn't Charles make a grand go of it?" said John. "Egad! When he said this was the proudest day of his life, I couldn't help crying out hear! hear! myself and then *I* spoke, too, between whiles. I thought I saw your ladyship waving your handkerchief at both of us."

"Indeed, I did," returned Julia, whose laughing eyes sparkled like stars, for she was now completely in her element. "Indeed, I did, and I would have waved all the banners on the field if it had been in my power. Two primer cracks[90] I never either heard or saw. It was heart-stirring. Why, gentlemen, eloquence like yours might persuade a person to do anything—hanging, drowning, shooting would all seem easy enforced by such fine, flowing language. I must beware, truly I must, it's dangerous!"

"O not a pin, not a bit of it. Nothing can be dangerous to your ladyship. I've a good mind to present you my pointer Dash, the finest that ever ran on the Warner Hills, in token of gratitude."

"Aye, do, Charles. It'll be to the hollor of the family that we should appear generous and to act in a manner becoming a gentleman. I don't care if I add that brace of fine ferrets Stitch and Sting 'at you know did such slaughter last spring in Richard Agar's rabbit warrens. He never forgave them for beating his pitiful rattons."[91]

"No more he did, John. And our Henry took his side—more shame to him!"

"Aye, Charles! And our Romilly lost five gold Adrians[92] that same ferret match."

"Yes, and your George won them!"

"Yes, and he spent them on a dozen of Madeira, and your William bolted four bottles."

"Yes, and your James could only make away with two."

"Aye, and he spewed half of them up afterwards."

I know not how long these edifying reminiscences would have continued, had not Edward Percy's ringing voice interrupted them.

"Silence there!" said he. "Not a word out of your heads till I've done speaking."

"My lords, ladies and gentlemen, I invite every soul of you this night to Edwardston Hall. The sun has set, the town clock has struck six, and the carriages are waiting, so make haste."

Now began the simultaneous movement through all the amphitheatre-like stage. The ladies rose in a body. Such a waving of plumes and curls, such a glitter of eyes and diamonds, I never before beheld. Their husbands, beaux and brothers stood ready to hand them to their chariots. I saw Julia trip laughing along with Thornton on one side of her, Charles on the other, and John, to whom she had entrusted her fan and pocket handkerchief, following behind. All at once, in the midst of some brilliant sally, a cloud of thought darkened her lovely face. It passed in an instant, but what occasioned it? Was she thinking of Sydney?[93]

"Cecillia," said Maria Percy, turning to her sister-in-law whose gentleness, contrasted with her own high-spirited pride, she is very fond of, "will you come with us? Do, love!"

A young fair-haired man stepped forward and hastily drew my cousin's arm through his. "Not so, madam," he said bowing, "My wife should be welcome to accompany you, but she cannot be a guest at my brother's house."[94] He moved away.

In half an hour's time, the long, long train of vehicles had all rolled in vast procession from the field, and they could be seen in the fading light sweeping up Stuartville Road, diminishing momently till the hindmost loiterer vanished and the faintest sound of wheels died to silence.

I too had quitted the place of meeting, but it was in an opposite direction, and now I sat two miles from the City Hall—two miles from Zamorna, at the gate of a peaceful and elegant mansion surrounded by tall elms and smooth sloped lawns (not parks) with rose-trees and laburnums shading the dewy grass, all calm around me—the moon rising, the sky cloudless, the stars looking dimly out, a wind as faint as thought whispering fitfully in the scarce-stirred leaves, the lights of the illuminated town twinkling far off and its subdued noise and clashing bells heard like a mountain torrent. I was within the precincts of Elm Grove Villa,[95] formerly Lily Hart's place of romantic seclusion, when Zamorna was an unfrequented village and the country round as solitary as it is now populous. Captain William Percy purchased this mansion of Fidena shortly after his marriage and has resided there ever since.

Soon a sound of approaching steps aroused me from a reverie into which I had fallen. I looked up. A group of four or five persons was slowly advancing up the long cornfield which stretches from the garden gate. They crossed the hawthorne shaded stile and stood before me. I was rather astonished to recognize in the foremost Major Albert Howard's tall grand figure. Two ladies, in whose fine Roman features, yellow hair, snowy skins and haughty blue eyes I knew Georgiana and Eliza[96] Seymour, leaned on his arm and both seemed as emulous of his notice as in their royal pride they usually appear careless of all other men's. They addressed him by the name of Augustus and not that of Albert or Howard. Captain and Lady Percy followed after.

Cecillia saw me. "Well, Charley," said the sweet creature, taking my hand and leading me forward, "are you come to pass the night at my house? You see I have a small but select party. Georgiana and Eliza came yesterday and they will stay a week. Have you spoken to them yet, child?"

"Not I! And if I did they'd only just pat my head. The girls seem to be entirely taken up with that Apollonic Mars, Major Howard. Is he married, pray?"

"A widower," said William Percy, "with five or six children."

"Five or six! Why, what years has the man numbered?"

"Never mind, sir. I'd advise you not to come near him. He's very passionate."

We entered the house by a glass door which admitted us at once to the drawing-room, which was glimmering in parlous twilight, shed from the brilliant and cheering hearth.

Major Albert threw himself on the sofa in a very easy quite-at-home sort of way. "Here, girls," said he to my noble cousins, "get the footstools and be seated. I've made the sofa my own." And to prove this unceremonious appropriation, he stretched his long limbs on the velvet couch and rested his curled head on its cushions. The ladies Seymour took the lowly seats he had appointed them, and, with their flowing robes spread on the rich carpet, sat with the grace and air of Persian princesses at his side. Young Percy leaned over the sofa back.

"Cecillia," said he, "how that scoundrel Edward would envy me if he knew what a treasure I have in my villa! Your Majesty, Elm Grove is a fairer place than Edwardston?"

"A calmer place," remarked the Major, "and, therefore, after a day of turmoil, far preferable. Now, William, get your flute. Cecillia, fairy, there stands the harp and there the music book. Georgiana, is that a guitar lying in the recess? Eliza, that grand piano woos your fingers.[97] We'll have an evening of peace and harmony. For myself I do nothing but lie and listen."

I was sorry that night when twelve o'clock chimed from the bronze timepiece on the sideboard. An evening of stiller and deeper enjoyment I never passed; it will ever remain a sunny spot on the chequered path of life.

[IV. *In which Lord Charles enters the palace and observes the Duke of Zamorna in his domestic capacity.*]

It was ten o'clock on the night subsequent to the one I last described that myself, General Thornton, Lord Castlereagh, Mr Edward Percy and Major Albert Howard arrived at Adrianopolis by the Conqueror mail coach,[98] a mode of travelling *en passant* much in vogue with the Angrians and usually preferred by them to their private carriages.

We alighted at the Plume and Sabre Hotel. Major Howard did not enter. He paid his fare and, envelloping himself in a large scarlet roquelaure,[99] mingled with the gas-lit[100] crowd on the causeway. I marked in what direction he strode along and followed with close and wary steps. He took a strangely circuitous route through narrow lane, blind alley, close, wynd[101] and covered passage. Adrianopolis seemed known to him through all its darkest and lowest details. I felt as if wandering in an utterly unknown wilderness, but, guided sometimes by his Saul-like figure[102] and sometimes, when gloom rendered that invisible, by his equal and ringing tread, I contrived to dog him with tolerable pertinacity. We emerged suddenly from a long dim lane to the glory of a wide serene, unbroken expanse of moonlight, slumbering on a proud, white pile, which towered about two hundred yards in front.

At first the scene that burst so unexpectedly on my vision only inspired vague ideas of boundless grandeur, but soon I was able to take a calmer and more careful view. What seemed solemn, vast, undefined, as the hoary cone of Caucasus ere long settled down into an edifice of mason's work. It stretched indeed far away and ascended to a sublime height, but still its limits were well and clearly outlined. A mighty row of marble pillars, pale and gleaming as ice, receded in their grand perspective before me. Their eternal basements, their grand shafts, their gorgeous capitals, the long, long, high-uplifted cornice that ran above them, were all of the purest, the noblest Grecian moulding. All breathed of Ionia in her loftiest times. Here the hand of that great architect Palladio could not be seen. The Venetian's classic elegance had given place to a profounder, a sterner, a more imperial style. Aye, the Zamorna Palace contrasted with Wellesley House shews well how the lord of both has changed and risen. Once he was the man of taste, learning, genius, science, at once the Homer and the Maecenas of his age;[103] *now*—but I will not waste time and temper by writing what he *now* is.

Beyond the palace, the Calabar was rolling all its broad smooth billows. I heard them kiss the marble walls as they swept on, as if doing homage to him who had thus glorified the shores which were once wild as a wilderness.

Major Howard crossed the silent square. He did not ascend the vestibule, but stole very softly round a wing of the edifice and stopped at a private door before which a sentinel was pacing. "Stand!" said the man, as that tall shadow-like form approached.

"Arise,"[104] was the brief reply. Instantly the musket rung reversed on the pavement, and its bearer drew back with an air of profound reverence.

"William Chadwick, I think," said Howard.

"The same, Your Majesty."

"John Ingram is your partner on the watch tonight, is he not?"

"Yes. Your Majesty knows us all!"

"By name I do. Good evening, William. A fine starry night."[105]

He touched the call-bell, which returned a faint silver sound. The door instantly unclosed and he entered. I lingered a moment behind. Through the open door I saw Eugene Rosier disencumbering him of the roquelaure.

"Will your lordship have a change of dress now or not?" he asked.

"No, it signifies little. Where is your lady, Rosier?"

"In the purple saloon, I believe, my lord. She gave Mr Robert Sdeath an audience there half an hour since."

"Sdeath! Hum! Scoundrel! What can his business have been?"

With these words he walked away. I followed, of course opposed by neither the sentinel nor Eugene, both happening to be well acquainted with me. Creeping up the little marble staircase, which terminated a small but elegant hall, I presently entered a long lamp-lit, sounding, lonely corridor. I think few but the Major would have ventured to wake such an echo as did his brass-shod boots in abodes so regally, so grandly silent. He turned off soon into the interior chambers, and after him I wandered through such a suite of rooms, bewilderingly magnificent and all the more impressive from the light which revealed them—soft, solemn moonshine pensively stealing through the Grecian windows and tinting with pearl and silver whatsoever its lustre touched.

He paused at the folding doors of one apartment, opened them gently and without again entirely closing them, went in. They were just sufficiently ajar to allow me a full view of the penetralia.[106] Here warm lights were glowing over the rich deep sombre hangings, dazzling carpets, and Tyrian couches. Queen Mary Henrietta appeared in the midst alone, alone (as Julia Sydney says), partially reclined on the piled cushions of a purple silk ottoman, beautiful, delicate as a dream, all fair and soft and tranquil and imperial.

Aye! I now felt I was in a king's palace. The host of loveliness which dazzled me so at Zamorna faded away; they were people of this world, who went in flocks, and laughed and talked and jested socially. But this was a clear, large star of beauty,[107] appropriated and dwelling apart in its own cloudless quarter of the sky—a priceless pearl which a strong man[108] had found and which he kept and guarded jealously. Yet royal as was Queen Mary's solitude, it appeared likewise melancholy. I did not envy her. She seemed cut off by greatness from commerce with her kind. Still, the haughty expression of her brow and of her beaming moonlight eyes told it was no matter of regret to her. Happy, however, she was not, but pensive, mournful, disconsolate, and as she impatiently turned her cheek on the cushion which supported it, and veiled her forehead with her hand, the tears of some secret sorrow trickled through these slender fingers.

An ebony table stood at her side on which lay an unfolded paper, and there her eye seemed to linger with intense anxiety. Major Albert fixed on her a long and steadfast gaze. Ere he withdrew it she looked up and saw him. The convulsed start with which she sprang

the tears of some secret sorrow trickled through these slender fingers.

up from her couch bespoke an overwrought mind. For a moment she stood bewildered. The disguise had scattered her ideas. One word however—her own name, Mary,[109] whispered in a low tone and accompanied by a gentle smile—sufficed to complete the recognition. She did not run forward, but said softly and sadly, "Ah, Zamorna, did you think *I* could be blinded by a mask like that? Where have you been, my lord, and how long is it since you went? I scarcely know how time passes."

The Duke curled his lips, walked to the fire, and was silent. Just then he actually, for once in his life, felt displeased with himself.

The Duchess spoke again. "Do tell me where you have been, Adrian, I only want to know that."

"What ails you, Henrietta?" said he quickly.

"I am very sorrowful as I have been for a long while now."

Zamorna's hand went to the gold chain across his bosom and he looked as gloomy as night.

"Am I to have the old story?" he said, glancing at her and then letting his eye fall—a dismal look that scarcely seems of earth, earthy.[110] She did not reply and he went on, "Sdeath has been with you, has he not?"

"He has, my lord."

"And what was the fiend's errand?"

He came from my father, sire."

"That I did not doubt! He is ever the messenger of Satan![111] And what said he of thy father, Dove?"

"That his health and spirits drop more in a foreign country than they did at home. He likewise brought this letter, which I would offer Your Majesty, only I fear —"

"Fear nothing, child. It cannot contain sentiments more infernal than those I give him credit for, so let us see the precious document."

"I trust, sire, you will think more favourably of my father when you have seen his heart there disclosed," said Henrietta as she gave the paper to her husband. He sat down. The shaded lustre dependent from the saloon ceiling gave his light. With compressed lips and settled aspect he perused Northangerland's famous letter to the Angrians. Not a sound interrupted the silence which reigned around while the Duke was thus employed, except the rustling sheets as he turned them over.

Mary watched him intently. With an unconscious movement she stole by degrees nearer to him till she stood at his side. Then, weary of standing, she kneeled on one knee and, resting against his sofa, looked up into her lord's face with so fond, so tender, so appealing an expression, that nothing I have seen either in sculpture or painting could equal the feeling of pathos it conveyed.

He concluded and laid the paper down. His cheek had become brightly flushed towards the end, and his eyes were assuming an excited and flashing glow.

"Sire, may I speak?" asked the Queen, clasping her hands with earnestness.

He heard her voice but I think not her words. His spirit was far off in another region, and, regarding her surpassing loveliness with a faint abstracted smile, he gathered his energies in profound thought.

Mary took the smile for consent and, drawing still closer, she addressed him thus: "I know, sire, you will now with your own kingly candour confess that Lord Northangerland means you no harm. He calls Zamorna his noble king and warmly declares his admiration of him. Oh, Adrian, if you knew how much I love my father, you would appreciate the sufferings I have lately endured! I saw your aspect darken whenever he passed before you. I knew you hated him and I never spoke a word. I bade him farewell—it might be for the last time. I watched the vessel that bore him from Africa lessen and vanish and I still kept silence. I heard on all sides hints thrown out that the Queen had no influence, or that she was coldly apathetic—so my brother Edward taunted me to my face, and I endured this also.

Hardest of all, sire, I feared—was it without reason?—that your dislike of Percy began to mingle with your feelings towards his wretched daughter. I wept alone and, though my heart nearly broke with the unnatural effort, I laid my finger on my lips still. I had a reason for this conduct which I scarcely dared whisper to myself. It was the appalling dread that Your Majesty's aversion might be well founded—that Percy might in truth be Zamorna's bitter foe; and whether right or wrong, just or impious, I stood prepared to sacrifice my father's very life, truly as I loved him, to the interests of him whom I could not help adoring with blind, infatuated, consuming zeal. My own life, my own happiness I will not speak of—they seemed as dust in the balance.[112] But, sire, when two hours since I received that letter, when I had read it, the delusion at once passed away. I knew then that Northangerland was true to you, and I blessed him with my whole soul for it. My father has been wronged, sire, vilely and wickedly wronged. He has human feelings but a superhuman intellect. Errors may have resulted from this incongruity, and these, he says, he will not defend, and after that noble confession who shall dare to accuse him? My king, my husband, my very deity, smile at me once more, and tell me that Percy shall again be your right hand! O sire, he is worth all the jackals that throng round you now. He is a true and royal lion worthy to consort with yourself, while his detractors are inferior to the dust your foot has prest. Am I to lie down on a sleepless pillow tonight Zamorna? Am I to eat the bread and drink the waters of bitterness, or, blessed with the forgiving light of your countenance, am I to sleep in peace and awake in safety?"[113]

Her enthusiasm as she knelt almost crouched in her earnest pleading at his feet, her sweet and swelling tones, her whole aspect, like Philippa supplicating for the Calaisians or Esther[114] for the devoted Hebrews, quickly recalled Zamorna's absent thoughts, and he heard the latter part of her prayer with deep attention. The monarch's hand shook through the influence of some strong internal emotion as he passed it over his broad white brow and then let it slowly fall on his queen's head bowed before him like a storm-beaten lily. She burst into happy tears the moment she felt his fingers laid caressingly on her golden curls.

"Be calm, love, be calm, my dear Mary," said he in that still, dew-like voice of his which Lord Richton has well characterized as being like the flute-stop of an organ. "I would indeed receive your father back with open arms, for his gentle daughter's sake, if sincerity had prompted one-fourth part of the sentiments his letter contains—but no, Mary, I see nothing like the light of truth. One hollow wheel turns with a still hollower, and all the mass of machinery weaves together a veil of deceit that might blind Machiavel's eyes, but I have cast it from me and I'll walk my own path steadfastly, turning neither to the right hand nor the left."

Mary sighed deeply. "Am I never to see my father again then?" said she.

"I trust you will, love, and in this very palace. I even prophesy that before a month passes he will be Premier of Angria again. It is my determination to throw no obstacles in his way. His genius, so grandly develloped in that letter, I want, and if possible I will have it. But by God's help I will beware of his insidious wickedness!"

"He loves you, sire," again interposed Henrietta. The Duke smiled. He gently raised his wife and, having placed her on his own sofa, began himself to pace the room with folded arms and thoughtful forehead. His quickened step soon shewed that the current of his meditations was running high and strong.

He paused. Mary looked at him. There he stood with the red firelight flashing over him, one foot advanced, his head proudly raised, his kindled eyes fixed on the opposite wall and filled with a most inspired glory. That tinge of insanity[115] which certainly mingles with his blood was looking through their fierce dilated zones,[116] as if it glared out at visions which itself had poured through the air.

"We walk together," he exclaimed aloud. "Our hands shall be twined; our purposes must be one. He has no heart and I'll rend mine from my bosom before its quick hot pulsations shall interfere with what I see, with what I feel, with what I anticipate by day and night. Why else were we born in one century? His sun should have set before mine rose, if their blended shining was not destined to set earth on fire. By the great Genii, it spreads! What! Farther, farther, a deeper, longer, gorier vista! I'll follow. You dare not beckon where I dare not go. Hah! It is stopped, filled up. Blackness, blackness, where am I? The day went down suddenly! All is utterly dark. Spirit! Percy! I have seen the end of my battles. How time hastens—twenty years did you say?—gathered in the span as at this distance it seems of one hour. Life slides from under me and there is the gulph of eternity. Eternity! Deep, bodiless, formless. What sails there? Why is there no sound? Such a stony silence; such a desolate vacancy. There should have been stars in the space. Who said I might remember? A vain hope! Thought slips already. Earth, existence, I have been great in both, but I remember no more my greatness." He ceased. His eyes had become fixed, his face looked ashen and lifeless, but with one hand on his breast and the other resting on a stand of lamps he still stood rigidly upright.

While he spoke my attention had been too much absorbed to notice what passed at the other end of the saloon, but now I heard a voice say, "You have seen him so before, Mary?"

I looked round. A gentleman in black stood beside the Duchess, and his powdered hair and sternly statuesque physiognomy at once announced the Duke of Wellington.[117] He wore a travelling dress and had evidently only just arrived at the palace. Mr Maxwell Senr accompanied him; his tall professional figure appeared in the background.

Henrietta seemed calm and collected, only she trembled all over. "I have seen the Duke so twice before," said she. "Both times then I was alone and I never spoke a word of it to any living creature. Was Your Grace aware of these paroxysms?"

"Aye, aye, Mary, and stranger ones than these, or at least more dangerous. Is Alford in the house?"

"Yes, but I beg Your Grace will not send for him. Zamorna is not senseless now. He would be infuriated by the slightest movement towards the bell or door. I committed that mistake once and I shall never forget the tone and look with which he commanded me to desist."

"Humph," replied my father. "Like a possessed corpse, I suppose. Maxwell, your young master is at times a real demon."

Maxwell shook his head. "Shall I send for William?" he whispered. "He attended the Duke at Philosopher's Island, when his mind, being troubled about Lady Victorine,[118] was frequently shaken in this way."

"Send for no one, I tell you!" said Mary quickly. "I will venture to approach him myself, if you dare not, Maxwell. It was not Lady Victorine whom he saw now, though her spirit once stood between me and him. I say no man on earth knows what those have to suffer, who, idolizing Zamorna as I do, see him in his dark moments. I verily believe he has revelations which other people have not, or else his imagination is burning as a hot coal. But look! He moves. I'll go to him."

She was about to approach, but the Duke of Wellington placed his strong sinewy arms round her and held her firmly back.

"Be still, my love," said he. "I would not trust him at this moment."

Zamorna slowly paced the saloon and then he drew towards that group. I was glad just then I did not form a part of it. He stopped within half a yard of them, and fixed upon them such an aspect, such eyes—it was evident he saw neither his father, his wife, nor Maxwell. The organs of vision were still and glazed;[119] they looked through and beyond all solid objects, with motionless intensity—motionless except an occasional flittering of the eyelid and long lashes. They watched the transient visions imagination had pourtrayed, then they turned slowly upwards. His face whitened more and more.

Something like foam became apparent on his lip, and he knitted his brow convulsively.

The Duke of Wellington turned to Maxwell. "Carry my daughter from the room," he said. "Never mind how she struggles, and return yourself instantly."

The steward having obeyed these orders, my father in turn closed and locked the three doors of the apartment, not omitting the folding door, and so, my post of observation being destroyed, I saw no more.

[V. *In which news of an opportune death reaches the Duke.*]

"Father, you here?" said the Duke of Zamorna, as he entered his lady's breakfast-room on the following morning, to all appearance quite well, only that a slight trace of exhaustion lingered on his features. "When and how did you come? What brought you? But I can guess. Was it not Northangerland's letter?"

The Duke nodded gravely.

"Well," continued his son, "I have given that matter due consideration and here is the result of my reflections." He handed my father a written sketch of the speech which he afterwards delivered at the opening of the Angrian Parliament.

"When did you write this?" asked Wellington, when he had perused it.

"Last night!"

"Last night, my boy? Impossible! Are you aware of your own state at that time?"

"My state! My state!" said Zamorna hurriedly as if recalling some disagreeable association.

"Oh, I suppose—I feared it, for on awaking at midnight I could recollect nothing, nothing about the evening. And you were there—My God! I trust no one else. Was Mary? Yes, yes—one look is enough: pale and harrassed. Bless thee, Henrietta, I shall wear you out soon—as I did—Hem![120] It is not my will—I cannot help it." He blushed and sorrowfully leaned his head on his hand. Mary looked fondly at him. She would have risen from her seat, but my father stopped her by changing the subject.

"I came to Adrianopolis partly on private business," said he, "and we'll talk of that now and leave the public till after breakfast. Augustus, read that." He took a letter from his pocket-book and threw it across the table. It was directed, "To His Grace the most noble Arthur Augustus Adrian, Duke of Zamorna, King of Angria, etc.", and its contents ran as follows:

My lord Duke,

It is with regret I inform you of the removal of my honoured master. His Highness the Duke Badhi expired suddenly yesterday afternoon. He was sitting down in his chair by the fireside, when the pipe which he held in his hand dropped out and his face turned quite black. Monsieur Designats, who was making his usual call, proceeded to offer every assistance, but without avail. Life was extinct. M.D. pronounces apoplexy to have been the cause of my lord's death. He wished to open the body. I, of course, thought it my duty to oppose any such intention, at least until I had communicated with Your Grace. The will is in my hands. I have transmitted a copy of it to William Maxwell Esqr by the post. Should Your Grace think proper to give personal orders respecting the funeral, Badhi Palace stands completely prepared to receive yourself and suite. Otherwise I shall be happy to act under the guidance of Mr Maxwell. I have as yet sent no intelligence of this truly lamentable event to the castle in Humeshire, since I think Your Grace formerly expressed a desire to correspond on all subjects by autograph with the Lady Frances Millicent Hume, and doubtless the blow will fall lighter when received through your medium. Resting always

Your Grace's most obliged, humble and obedient servant,

I am,

Mildert O'Sullivan.

P.S. This morning I took legal opinion respecting the forms to be observed in case Your Grace should think proper to change the title from Duke of Badhi to Duke of Alderwood, as you once intimated you would do. Sir Copley Lyndhurst[121] informed me that the payment of five hundred pounds, into your royal father's exchequer, and as much into that of Verdopolis, is all that the law requires to complete such an alteration.

"Well," said Zamorna when he laid down the letter, "that's good news, though it be of death! And very decently handled, O'Sullivan. No congratulation. Right! What smooth tongues these stewards have! That's as like what Maxwell would have written as need be. Hum, so His Highness Alexander Badhi has at last smoked his final pipe, drunk his final pint, and cut his final subject. Old Doit,[122] I am sorry he went with such little warning. Should like to have seen his death-bed—it would have been a sorry one. Scolding and cursing the attendants —"

"Well, sir," said my father, interrupting this very indecent strain of comment, "is that all you have to say about a man who has left you two hundred thousand pounds sterling per annum?"

"Pretty near," was the reply. "But, father, a curious question has entered my head. Where is he gone? Upwards or downwards? He's not fit for heaven, and yet, dotard and brute as he was, Lord Northangerland's master's fireside seems too warm for him. 'I should be wae to think on it for his sake.'[123] There must be an intermediate receptacle of Hades, as I always said."

Here he took out his pocket-book and wrote: "Mem: to poze Stanhope next after-dinner sitting with a new argument on my favourite point. Badhi: *imprimis*, his life and conversation; *secundum*, his death and salvation. Beat him last time—shall crush him this!"

"Father," he continued, "how shall I order the burial? Splendid I suppose, he being one of the Twelves?"[124] And the royal scapegrace hemmed significantly.

"As you like, sir, but be more decent, I tell you! Come with me. I ordered the Maxwells to await us in your study."

"I'll come. Good morning, Mary. I know I shall not have time to see you again till afternoon. Curse business! Get a mourning dress, love, as fast as you can. We must all go into deep, deadly funeral black, for no earthly reason except that we have got a new title, and new fortune. However, my Mary's fair face will look lovely in its black veil. There's a kiss, and again, good morning, Duchess of Zamorna, Duchess of Alderwood, Queen of Angria, and I know not what besides."

He left the room. "Bless his noble heart," murmured Henrietta.

"And his whirling brain," added my father, who followed directly after.

As they entered the study they were greeted by the low bow and the muttered salutations of the Maxwells, Junr and Senr. Zamorna stopped in the doorway and fixed on them his sparkling and piercing eye (rather different now to what it was twelve hours since, when his imagination had so taken the reins of his reason that both were nearly driven to death).

"Now, most worthy crocodiles,[125] alligators of house and land," said he, "which of you is best prepared to condole with me on the afflicting loss I have sustained? William, thy yellow face seems best prepared. Such immovable rigidity of muscle! Look at him, father: the eyebrows gently corrugated, the face lengthened precisely to the measure of Paganini's fiddle,[126] the corners of the mouth drawn down, the complexion more ochrey than usual, as if grief had produced a suffusion of bile,[127] the black locks streaking the swarthy temples with Nature's own mourning. O thou art all comely to look upon: a dewy rose of Sharon, a weeping lily of the valley![128] My dear William—my Jonathon, my Pythias, my Pylades, or rather my Joab, my Achates, my Patroclus[129]—dry thy tears. Tomorrow for more melting thought. But now to business. Where's the will?"

"Your Grace is aware that I have not the original," replied Mr William gravely, "only the copy indorsed by Mr O'Sullivan. Shall I read it aloud?'

And he produced a huge parchment packet, tied, sealed and folded with official scrupulosity.

"Don't read it at all, sir! Give it to your father and let him read it to my father. As for you, come here. Sit down at that desk and write what I shall dictate. Direct to Mildert O'Sullivan Esqr, steward to the Alderwood Estates etc. Commence.

"'Sir, the Duke of Zamorna directs me to express the deep concern he feels in your intelligence of yesterday's date.'

"Written that? It's every word true, mind! I do feel very deeply concerned.

"'He desires the funeral may be conducted on a magnificent scale suitable to the rank of the illustrious deceased and —'

"Make haste! How you shuffle, William! 'And that invitations be issued to such of the surviving Twelves as are not non compos mentis'.[130]

"Craki, and our venerable patriarch, David Crachi, being by that proviso excluded. Write, sir! What are you bungling about? 'So'—leave nothing out —'the carriages at Wellesley House, those at Waterloo Palace, will make part of the funeral train. A detachment will likewise be sent from Adrianopolis. I have my lord's command to intimate that he will himself take the post of chief mourner as being heir to the title, etc. My lady will not attend. It is His Grace's purpose to continue you in the stewardship, and the inferior domestics will likewise remain unchanged. I am, sir,

Your obedient humble servant,

Wm Maxwell'

"Now have you finished? Aye that'll do. There's a more decent epistle than you would have concocted, and not an atom of falsehood. Vacate! The next epistle must be an autograph."[131]

Mr Maxwell left the escritoire and His Grace, assuming the steward's seat, took another sheet of paper and wrote rapidly as follows:

Well Millicent, love, I believe, after all, your kind little heart will be rather grieved when I tell you that he who should have been your father died a day or two since of apoplexy. You must only shed one tear, though, and heave one sigh. More would be utterly superfluous. He has not even mentioned your name in his will, which, by a sweeping clause, throws every stiver of the property into my all-grasping hands. But I'll see you well cared for, my sweet cousin. Not a blast of cold wind shall come near you. Aye, Augustus is your father now, and your brother and guardian, too, Milly. I know my little blind orphan will feel an added desolation when this news arrives, but if I could tell it with my own voice, in my own person, not a tear should fall, or the hand that now writes should quickly wipe it away if it did.

Where would you best like to live, Frances? At the castle or the old lodge, or Mornington Court,[132] or the palace, or Wellingtonstown?[133] Perhaps none of these please you. I remember a sadly intimated wish in your last letter that you were nearer to Zamorna, who employs far more of your thoughts than he deserves. Well then, love, shall I build you a little fairy pavillion[134] on the banks of a bright stream which I have christened the Arno, running through Hawkscliffe Forest,[135] along a tiny green valley of its own? I see the smile with which you would welcome this proposal, and it shall be done. Effie Lindsay will read you this letter. Tell her to be as good as she is bonny[136] and get on with her music, etc., so as to be able to sing me "Jessy the flower o'Dunblane" when I next see her, and she shall follow her mistress to the east. My foster-mother will sit upon the ancient threshold under the ancient roof-tree.

I remain, Millicent,
Ever thine,
Augustus Wellesley

* * * * * * * * * * * * * * *

[VI. *In which is found a mysterious document of unknown import.*]

Found the following on the Duke of Zamorna's study-table, between the leaves of a Greek book which he had been reading. It is an odd, wild fragment. Interpret it for me who can.

Scene: *Moonlight, a Palace Balcony, Adrianopolis in the distance, Zenobia solus.*

Zen[*obia*]: Fair, placid, tranquil—such are the epithets commonly applied to moonlight. At this moment I do not feel them to be just. The moon looks strangely wild tonight. Red as blood, though she is ten degrees above the horizon. She hangs over the city threateningly, with her large dim halo portending a storm ere long. Yonder is a bark on the Calabar, outward bound, as I think. Let the mariners beware. Hah! I saw the ship, but now, where is it? Gone! The shadow of a cloud obscured its white twinkle, and that cloud, having darkened the glancing river, now floats above Adrianopolis. It passes, passes, passes. One tower, one dome, one palace and street and square after another lapse in the gloom, are hidden, look out again, pallid as sheeted ghosts. The cloud has flitted on—or is that it lying like a black dim line along the horizon? No, no, only its shade palling the Zamorna Hills. But it rolls up. Their sides are bathed in silver, both sky and earth are once more clear.

Why have I watched the course of a wreathed pile of vapour so intently? I know not. My mind has been in a strange mood all day and is so still at eventide. I would fain fix it on somewhat, but it will remain steady nowhere. Detached fragments of the past, the long past, the never to return, have since morning been gliding through my memory like that cloud. And still as they vanished one haunting fancy remained behind, and what is it? A foolish one, but I cannot think it unfounded: that I had something to do before midnight, some important and solemn duty to perform. I know not its nature. I only feel the impression, and that at times is so strong that I have started from my seat in urgent horror.

Once I thought the fleeting mystery was caught. When walking in the picture gallery at noon, my Alexander's portrait caught my eye. It vivified,[137] as it often does when I am alone and thoughtful, into life, flesh and existence. Though dead, he yet lived. The eye looked at me so strangely. A melancholy, a warning, a commanding light filled it and inspired it, till I trembled with the marvellous reality of the likeness. Then a recollection rushed on, of what I had said, what I had promised, long, long since. I tried to keep and unfold it. I gasped with eagerness. I gazed again and again on the picture that it might enlighten me, but vainly, all died off. Alexander's form was no longer the one I had known and loved, but only its faint representation, and for the remembrance, that became more vaguely indefinite than ever.

Hush! I hear a step.

(*enter Alpha*[138])

Alph: Zenobia! You here! And alone! It is cold, dark and wants but half an hour of midnight.

Zen: My lord, may I not say the same to you?

Alph: Aye! But then I have a reason for coming, a reason such as night and solitude best suits. The wind sounds doleful this evening, Zenobia.

Zen: It does, but what is your reason, Alpha?

Alph: A strange one. Carry your thoughts twenty-one years back, Countess. On such a night, at such an hour as the present, did you promise nothing to one now dead, buried, and it may be mouldered away?

Zen: Ah! Are you come to solve the enigma? Since morning light I have been pondering on that promise, but what it is I know not.

Alph: I will tell you. Looking over the papers in an escritoire which had long remained closed, I this day found a memorandum to the following effect:

"Septbr. 30th 1834. Spent the evening at Ellrington House. Zenobia, Percy and I had a singular conversation, concerning death and its sequents. We (i.e. Z and myself) promised, in case Northangerland died before us, to visit the vault and unclose the coffin where he lay twenty years subsequent to his dissolution."

Now what say you to that, Countess?

Zen: What I sought is found! The truth falls on my heart like ice.

Yet now I would fain turn my eyes from so ghastly a light. Ghastly did I say? Aye, so it is, but sublime likewise, Alpha?

Alph: Zenobia! I can read your thoughts. You doubt and tremble. The proposition is very awful; yet fear nothing, I am with you.[139] We must pay that we have vowed.[140]

Zen: I consent. Few things can shake me long. I'll see Percy once again, though I should never smile more.

Alph: Well resolved. You were always the very Empress of Women, Zenobia. Nature, in your case, mistook and placed a masculine soul in a feminine casket. There—clasp my hand and come.
(*Exeunt*)

Here the dramatic fragment breaks off and the subject is continued in some lines of lyrical poetry.[141]

The crypt, the nave, the chancel past,
His burial aisle is gained at last.
His burial aisle! Oh! what a moan
Comes mingled with that simple tone.
No proud roofs rise for Percy now,
For him no gleaming arches bow;
The bright saloon, the columned hall
Is changed for shroud, and vault and pall.
The palace lit with sunshine clear
Has passed for rayless grave and bier.
The hearth of his patrician home,
The concave of his gorgeous dome,
Have long forgot his voice, his tread.
They like himself lie stilled and dead.
  Pass on: the hush is mournful
And the air is faint and dim,
And we know that earth is tombed in sleep
And we feel that midnight's shadow deep
  Brood round us brown and grim.
  Yet fear not, lady! fear not.
  Why dost thou tremble so?
I hear the beatings of thy heart,
I see thee at each murmur start,
  However faint and low.
  There is nothing here to harm thee:
  The dead are stilled for aye,
And many a year has glided by
In calm and storm since living eye
  Shed on that bier its ray.

Let's stand awhile; all is most still,
Save when the vault dews, dank and chill,
Settled in drops on arch and wall,
Down tinkling to the pavement fall
And, save when some strange, transient sound
Just echoes far and faintly round,
Then dies away as it was born,
Vague, nameless, drearily forlorn.
The creaking of a coffin lid,
A tressel 'neath its burden slid,
A louder blast of the night wind swelling,
The distant clock from its tower knelling,
Though feeble sounds, yet shrill and deep
They fall, in these lone cells of sleep
Where, void of motion, vision, breath,
Our fathers lie, at rest, in death!
And is this Percy's dwelling place?
Is *this* the goal of his proud race?
After the mighty path he trode
Is this his fixed and last abode?
Great spirit! hast thou slumbered here
While round and onward rolled our sphere?[142]
Still measuring out the marks of time
With customed change of light and clime?
Hast thou lain stirless in this cell
While kings and empires rose and fell
And war's shrill trumpet-blast has rung
So many startled lands among,
While anguished wail and heart-wrung moan
Have followed that arousing tone
From those its parting echoes left
Of all they loved, for ere bereft.
Sometimes that noble storm of sound
Burst almost o'er the hallowed ground
Where, Percy! thy cold ashes lie
Beneath their marble canopy;
Where, journeying from their far-off home,
The wandering feet of pilgrims come,
And worshipping, their forms they bow
To greet thy urn with lip or brow.
Sometimes it murmured far away
As distant thunder peals decay.
Land unto land in answer spoke,
Defiance sounded, war awoke,

The very billows of the sea
Took up that awful harmony.
The roar of thine own element
Was with its chords of thunder blent.
Great rivers running to the deep
Its voice bore onward in their sweep,
Yet thou didst not awake!
A hundred plains were strewed with dead,
A thousand hills grew gory red:
Morn saw them blushing when she rose
And still they blushed at twilight's close.
The moon her rays of silver threw
To shine on drops of crimson dew,
And sleep and silence fell no more
As night looked down on wave and shore,
And battle's dogs of slaughter yelled,
Rolled her dread drums, her clarions swelled,
Naught could thy slumber shake.
No more thy voice the senate stilled;
No more thy taunt its victims chilled:
That voice was hushed, the harp unstrung
Whence once its deep, clear accents rung,
And the taunt, the stern denouncing word,
Forgotten, lost, in death unheard.
But years the while have ceaseless flown;
Each after each has come and gone.
Thy crimes, thy deeds, thy glories be
Recorded themes of history.
Thy tomb has grown a mighty shrine,
Thy name a feared yet worshipped sign.
The clouds that once around it lay
Frown faintly through the mellowing ray
That still from lapsing ages stealing,
The grandeur not the gloom revealing,
Has given a deep solemnity
To every line that speaks of thee.
Oh Percy! can I now behold
The face that pall and shroud infold?[143]
O can I raise that coffin lid
And look on what is 'neath it hid?
Can I the awful forehead see
That cere-cloth[144] hides so jealously?
And see it as at last it lay
When the sun went down on the dying day;

When myself beside thy pillow bending
Felt the dim shade of death descending;
And knew by voiceless sign and token
That the pitcher at the fount was broken,
That the cistern wheel had ceased its turning,
And the lamp of being quenched its burning,
That the golden cord, just loosened, quivered
And the silver bowl lay crushed and shivered.[145]
Thy death, it was so calm and still
That but for the silence and frozen chill
I should have thought a blessed sleep
Had fallen, thy pangs in rest to steep,
But gathering shadow on shadow told
That nothing lay there save an ashen mould;
That soul from the eye and the forehead was gone,
And the seal of its grandeur left lingering alone;
The streams were exhausted in Life's deep well
And gone was the mighty infidel!

Bride of his living breast, draw near,
Bend, lady, o'er thy husband's bier:
For ere the night lamps farther wane
We'll look on Percy's face again!
(*Lifts the coffin lid, curtain drops.*)

C. Brontë Octbr 8th 1834. 138 lines

[VII. *In which Angria celebrates a royal delivery.*]

Well, the Duchess of Zamorna has done it at last, and in right, good, dashing Angrian style. Her subjects are delighted. They absolutely worship her. It comes so properly up to their ideas, somewhat out of the common line, the thing accomplished, and a trifle to spare. Angria will have nothing trite. There must be flash and bustle and rising sunism about all her affairs, especially where the King is concerned. Well they have it!

On the 5th of October 1834, about twelve o'clock high-noon, I was sitting in the front drawing-room of Julia Place (General Thornton's new residence in Adrianopolis, gallantly christened after Lady Sydney) and watching the bright and fervid sun burning on the arrowy Calabar and the white marble or freestone buildings that line its banks, and the busy vessels that swung at anchor or bounded at full sail down its full deeply rushing stream.

All at once, without any sound of previous warning, the window before which I sat was shaken by a strong iron thrill of sound, at first too stunning to admit of comprehension. After a moment's intermission it burst or rung out again, and then I knew it to be the united peal of all the bells in the Cathedral of the Holy Trinity, in the Churches of St Abdiel, St John, St Cyprian,[146] and of the Apocalypse. Twelve times was that mighty crash repeated. Then the bonds of sound seemed loosened, the chain of union apparently burst with the violence of the concussion, and they rung abroad through the sunny and cloudless sky, filling its echos with so sweet, so exulting, so inspiring a strain, that instinctively I shouted hurrah and rushed from the house into the street. It was full of people. How they had gathered so quickly I know not. All were talking as fast and loud and elbowing their way as vigorously and unceremoniously as if each man was charged with a matter of life and death. Bets I heard were going fast, and all seemed to hang on the alternative "son or daughter, daughter or son", for such was the key-note that ruled the chaos or sound around me.

"What is the matter?" asked I of a stout, able-bodied Angrian who happened to stand near.

"Matter?" he replied. "Why man, our bonny Queen, God bless her, has been doing her duty to her husband, her King and her country: unto us a child is born.[147] Whether it be son or daughter we can't tell yet, but two soldiers of the Horse Guards have just ridden full gallop down Parliament Street in the direction of the batteries, with orders about the artillery. Ten salutes will be fired if it's a boy, you know, and only five if it be a girl. If do I say? There's no if about the matter: it must be a boy!" And with this characteristic asseveration he turned on his heel.

The batteries on the east bank of the Calabar are distinctly visible from the end of Julia Place. In that direction all eyes were anxiously turned. Ere long a flash of fire, a cloud of smoke, a long loud deepening roar, belched from the bristling line of cannons and rolled over the water, gave the first welcome to the royal stranger. Another, a third, a fourth, a fifth came and went. All the city rested in expectation. When the red balls of the sixth discharge at length fell and rebounded on the river's breast, Julia Place spoke in a shout to Parliament Street, Parliament Street roared huzza to Adrian Road, Adrian Road called to Palace Square, Palace Square sent the news in thunder over the quays, the Strand, and Northangerland Terrace. Adrianopolis, in short, rose in a living earthquake of exultation. Ten was numbered by the east battery—the appointed number. An interval of six or seven minutes ensued and, to the astonishment of all, the west battery caught up the dying echo and crash after crash rattled round the city till ten more salutes were numbered.

At this moment a gentleman on horseback dashed through the throng. It was General Thornton, his face full of glee and his eyes sparkling with pleasure. "Bravo Angrians!" exclaimed he, waving his hat round his head. "Fling up your caps, and your wigs, men. Here I am fresh from the Palace. Sich news I never heard the like for good! Twins, my lads! Twins! And both thriving, handsome, healthy boys. There's for you."

The crowds were actually convulsed with enthusiasm at this intelligence. I left them, darkening the sun with their headgear, leaping, roaring, and hurrahing like mad. During that day I visited the palace, but could find no rest for the sole of my foot.[148] All except the left wing, where the Duchess lay and which was closed against everyone but her immediate attendants, revelled in a storm of glorious confusion; messengers returning and going forth; orders issuing for universal rejoicings; for the opening of hotels and inns and ale-houses at His Majesty's expense.

Maxwell, whose grave face and solemn eyes sparkled on this

Adrianopolis, in short, rose in a living earthquake of exultation.

day as they never have done before or since, walked about as if on springs. "I have written letters to the west," said he, in answer to some remark of mine, "and all the country will, I am certain, kindle into one great bonfire at the news. Alderwood must rejoice. The castle there is to be crowded with the tenantry and gentry of Humeshire. It's many a year since it had such a warming. Hawksclifffe, here in Angria will spread light through the forest from end to end. I understand from Mr Steighton that Lord Northangerland has given him general orders for the regaling of the Percy tenantry on the occasion of his grandsons' birth. Mr Warner and Mr Kirkwall have done the same, and so, I believe, has Enara, for the country has now another two more stays to rest on. The Grand Chamberlain swears that Arundel shall reel to its very foundations. Castlereagh answers for Zamorna, and, as to Adrianopolis, it's already in the seventh heaven of triumph."

"What does the Duke think about the matter?" asked I. "Is he glad?"

"Why, Lord Charles," returned Maxwell, "my master, you know, is rather difficult to fathom sometimes. All last night and this day has he been shut up in his study, and nobody but the Earl his father-in-law, Lady Helen Percy and Doctor Alford have been admitted to speak with him until about half an hour after his children were born, when he sent for me, to give some written orders. I found him walking very restlessly up and down the room; Lord Northangerland sitting near the mantlepiece as sadly thoughtful as if death instead of life had been added to the house. Zamorna smiled at me as I entered and very condescendingly put his hand into mine. It trembled and felt cold. I offered my humble congratulations with heartfelt sincerity."

"'Thank you, William,' he said quickly. 'I hope the country will be as pleased as yourself. Quite in the Angrian style—two instead of one! Well, I am glad the matter is over at any rate.'

"He talked to me about five minutes longer, rather hurriedly, and his eyes shone as he spoke, with that fitful kind of light they always have when his feelings are much excited. His right hand never left the eyeglass chain and scarlet breast ribbon a minute. On the whole I believe he is well pleased."

I remained at the palace till nightfall, watching an opportunity to see the Duke of Zamorna, if it were only for a minute, but in vain. I heard his voice and step once in the corridor. His person, however, had vanished before I could obtain a glimpse of it. Yesterday my influence with Miss Sophia Graham and Miss Amelia Clifton, two of the Duchess's ladies, procured me a sight of the young princes. I entered their nursery on tip-toe. It is all hung with white and silver

I entered their nursery on tip-toe.

damask, and their cradle is veiled with white satin curtains silver fringed and tasseled.

I saw the little fairies through a thin web of point lace suspended above them. They are just like the Duke of Zamorna's other children:[149] delicate and beautiful as if made out of modelled wax, with tiny ringlets of pale brown hair on their small snowy foreheads, and their father's eyes gleaming, large, full and dark underneath. It is strange that hereditary feature should (like Northangerland's nose) be transmitted with such exactness. Ernest, Julius and the present pair of whelps all precisely alike in that particular. I understand they will be christened with much pomp and splendour next week. Mr Maxwell, an unerring authority, gave me their intended names, titles and those of their sponsors male and female.

The eldest, that is the Heir Apparent of Angria and Wellington's Land[150] by right of four or five minutes' seniority, will be called Victor Frederic Percy Wellesley, Marquis of Arno. Godfathers: John Duke of Fidena, the Earl of Arundel, Edward Percy Esqr, and General Thornton. Godmothers: Zenobia Countess of Northangerland and Edith Countess of Arundel.

The name of the youngest is Julius Warner di Enara Wellesley, Earl of Saldanha. Godfathers: Viscount Richton (by personal request of His Majesty), Viscount Castlereagh, Warner Howard Warner Esqr and Henri Fernando di Enara Esqr. Godmothers:[151] Lady Maria Percy and Harriet Viscountess Castlereagh. Dr Stanhope, Primate of the kingdom, will christen the Princes, assisted by Dr Porteous, Primate of Northangerland, and Dr Warner, Primate of Angria.

Charlotte Brontë Octbr 9th 1834

The following song is the production of that same unknown[152] to whom we owe "Sound the Loud Trumpets", and "Welcome Heroes."

It is entitled

HURRAH FOR THE GEMINI![153]

Hurrah for the Gemini!
Blessed be the Star!
That shone on the stream of the blue Calabar
When the hills of the east and the woods of the west
Bore light for their banner and flame for their crest,
As the wind its glad tidings exultingly blew
That if Rome had one monarch, our Angria has two!

Sons of an imperial line!
Welcome to your land and home!
Not at daylight's dark decline
Princes! is your advent come.
Not as the orb of nations fades,
Not as the deepening evening shades
Gather in starless gloom;
But at morning's primal flush,
Angria's bright, uprising day,
When her hills have caught the blush
Of the earliest, fairest ray,
And the path of the untravelled skies
Before in crystal clearness lies

A wide, a trackless way.
When her gilded woods are bending
To the morning's wind of might,
When her mountain floods descending
Catch the sunbeam, dazzling bright,
Flash the golden lustre given
Backward to the breaking heaven
In richer rays of light.
Princes! then to life you woke;
Then your father clasped his own,
Then the shout of welcome broke,
Harp was swept and bugle blown;
Then the deep Atlantic rung
As its flashing waters sprung
To thunder back that tone.
Angria's glad and bracing breeze
With your earliest breath you drew,
All her mightiest energies
Round and o'er your cradle blew.
Drink them children of a king!
Up to noble beauty spring
In heaven's fair light and dew.
With your God-like father's form
Catch his spirit, catch his might,
Then, albeit the battle-storm
Gather round us black as night,
Still its blasts we may defy,
Still our flag aloft shall fly,
Still shall Angria's burning sky
Smile its living light.
Conqueror, ruler shall she be,
Sovereign queen by land and sea,
Her watch-word shall be "victory",
Her glory, ever bright!

Hurrah for the Gemini! blessed be the star!
That shone on the stream of the blue Calabar
When the hills of the east and the woods of the west
Bore light for their banner and flame for their crest,
As the wind its glad tidings exultingly blew
That if Rome had one monarch, our Angria has two!

53 lines

Charlotte Brontë
Octbr 14th 1834

[VIII. *In which the heirs are christened with all suitable ceremony, and Lord Charles falls out of the window.*]

CHRISTENING AND PRESENTATION

Yesterday was the christening and presentation day. I witnessed both ceremonies. The former took place at noon in Trinity Cathedral. A grand imposing spectacle it was. The aisles and nave were filled with the nobility and gentry of Adrianopolis. The area round the font was kept clear by a division of the Horse Guards. The entrance of the great procession at the north door was announced by the choir and organ bursting out with "Lord now lettest thou thy servant depart in peace, for mine eyes have seen thy salvation."[154]

Up, two and two, came the mighty, dazzling train, headed by Their Royal Highnesses the Duke and Duchess of Fidena, the rest of the sponsors following in due order. As they advanced, the military unfolded to the right and left. The prelates drew towards the font. The organ swelled louder and deeper and the voices of the choristers rose with an harmonizing increase of power.

They slowly arranged themselves in their appointed places. Zamorna and Fidena stood side by side. The former looked almost as solemn and thoughtful as his friend. By degrees the deep hum of sound subsided.

Stanhope's fine emphatic voice commenced the baptismal service. Then Zenobia Countess of Northangerland, and Lady Maria Percy approached, both richly, resplendently attired, bearing in their arms that day's youthful candidates for admittance into the bosom of Holy Church. Those two magnificent women kneeling on the marble steps of the font presented their charges to Drs Porteous and Warner.

All at that moment was quite still, the organ hushed, the multitude silent as death. I cannot describe what an impression was produced on me when, as Stanhope sprinkled the consecrated water, I heard amid that vast edifice the faint, feeble cry of an infant, and then the soothing hushing whispers of the ladies as each received back her startled lamb—it was indescribable but very solemn. The twelve sponsors, having pledged their awful vow of renunciation and adoption,[155] all knelt down in the concluding prayer, the gentlemen bare-headed, and the ladies' plumes bowed in supplication. The rustling sweep of their arising was lost in the modulated thunder with which Greenwood rolled out "We praise Thee O God! We acknowledge Thee to be the Lord, all the Earth doth worship Thee etc."[156] As that died away, the rearranged procession glided along aisle and chancel. They passed out at the south entrance and the congregation broke up.

Five o'clock in the afternoon was the time fixed for the presentation, and Saldanha Park, that immense green plain stretching behind Zamorna Palace, the place in which the ceremony was appointed to be performed. Before half-past three, the whole slope downward to the Calabar presented one vast crowded amphitheatre, and the Calabar itself, where it rolls past the palace, was blackened with boats and barges. Sentinels were stationed at the park gates, and a troop of light horse attended to keep the populace in order, which regulation was the more necessary as His Majesty had ordered twenty eighteen-gallon casks of strong ale to be broached and distributed.

Bands of music, scarlet flags, ribbons etc., were not wanting, and more than once did those two favourite national anthems, "Sound the Loud Trumpets" and "Welcome Heroes", swell in tumultuous chorus from the grounds.

It was a bright, clear day. The sun shone with autumnal softness and brilliancy. The wind breathed just freshly enough to wave the glorious red banners and sway to and fro the grand groups of trees which towered isle-like above the fluctuating ocean of mortality. The roar of the Calabar was hushed in the louder roar of those who thronged its banks and darkened its waters. Nothing appeared silent, nothing solemn save the marble abode of royalty and that had only the external aspect of peace. Within all was flashing splendour, exhilarating bustle, princely festivity. The whole aristocracy of Adrianopolis were gathered in its saloons, and they shone as brightly as patrician beauty and more than eastern magnificence could make them.

Five o'clock came ringing from the city towers. It was echoed by a real Angrian roar of impatience. At length the palace portals unfolded, and, far within, the great hall of audience was seen stretching, crowded with rank and loveliness. Edward Percy and his radiant bride appeared in the very threshold. A little behind, the Countess of Northangerland's tall figure arose like an impersonation of female grandeur. Lady Helen Percy stood beside her, then the Viscountess Castlereagh, the Countess Arundel, Julia Montmorency, Lady Cecillia Percy and many, many others. Amongst the gentlemen, I looked in vain for Lord Northangerland. He was not there. Shaver afterwards told me that during the whole of that day he remained shut up in the regal gloom of Northangerland House, a prey to the profoundest melancholy.

But as the gates of the great entrance rolled back, a side door also unclosed. Two tall dark-haired ladies, Sophia and Frances Graham, glided out and, passing among the pillars of the vestibule, paused between the two huge central columns. Each, as she stood still, stretched to the full view of the multitude a small beautiful image clad in sweeping white robes, with great brown sparkling eyes, whose light shone from under the shade of ostrich plumes[157] drooping over them in snowy pendency. The unusual size of these orbs communicated a strange, rather wild expression to their faces whose features were otherwise delicately sweet.

The Angrians welcomed their infant princes with a shout loud as from numbers without number numberless. The bands struck up and the banners waved exultingly. And now somewhat darkened the door of the palace a crested figure "in stature taller than the sons of men."[158] It had risen on a sudden and, with a quick impetuous gesture, it descended the flight of steps and advanced to the lawn-like space kept clear in front.

"Well, Angrians, that's what heaven has sent you!" exclaimed Zamorna, pointing to his children. "They are yours as well as mine. I dedicate them from their birth. Being born for Angria's good, they must live for her glory, and die if need be for her existence. I rejoice in their creation for your sakes. I love them as much for their connection with the land whose sun is now shining on them, as I do for the blood that runs in their veins and the flesh which covers their bones, though that blood and flesh be my own or dearer than my own. If I could, Angrians, I would permit every individual man here present to bless my children with his embrace and benediction, but since that may not be I will place them in the arms of your acknowledged representative, and in his person all Angrians shall salute her princes."

He turned and approached the nurses. I think his little scions had scarcely seen him so near before, for as the lofty shade drew nigh, they clung without screaming but with a scared and astonished look to their female guardians. He smiled, and bending his head and proud mourning plumes over one of them, Victor Frederic, I think, kissed it, and saying something in a very soft voice, gently took it to his bosom. The small creature yet gave no note of disapprobation; its tiny cheek ever dimpled with an answering smile.

"Let Mr John Kirkwall advance," said the Duke. That gentleman came forward.

"Since," continued His Grace, "you are the true epitome of Angria, the concentrated essence of her feelings and sentiments, I commit to your arms my son and successor. Let him imbibe his country's noble spirit with the kiss that her elected gentleman shall give."

Sorry I am, reader, to announce that I can give no further description of the presentation. Just as Zamorna was delivering up his child, I unfortunately, in stretching out of a window of the palace where I had established myself and whence I had hitherto viewed the affair, lost my balance and fell down a perpendicular height of twenty feet. I was taken up for dead, and till next morning I continued in a state of utter insensibility.[159] Excuse this hiatus.

C A F Wellesley

October 14th 1834 —

C Brontë

ANNOTATIONS

Our debt to Christine Alexander is everywhere apparent, for her excellent text of *My Angria and the Angrians*, which we have used as our copy text, and her annotations to it, which have been enormously helpful. We also make frequent reference to her definitive critical study, *The Early Writings of Charlotte Brontë* (1983). Full reference to all works will be found in our "Works Cited," but for brief reference in the notes we use the abbreviations noted below.

CA = Christine Alexander
CB = Charlotte Brontë
ECB = *An Edition of the Early Works of Charlotte Brontë:* I (1987), II.i and ii (1991), by Christine Alexander
EW = *The Early Writings of Charlotte Brontë* (1983), by Christine Alexander
JE = *Jane Eyre*
MUW = *The Miscellaneous and Unpublished Writings of Charlotte and P.B. Brontë*
OED = *Oxford English Dictionary*
PCB = *The Poems of Charlotte Brontë and Patrick Branwell Brontë*
S = *Shirley*
V = *Villette*
WH = *Wuthering Heights*

1 **Angria:** Although CB refers to Angria in her manuscripts before Branwell does, his influence prevails. The battles in Branwell's narratives lead to these demands by Zamorna: "Hear me, Kings and Noblemen of Verdopolis … I have reconquered this City from the Enemies … Now, for these services rendered by me to my country, I demand from it the possession of my fields of Battle, … the Provinces of Angria, Calabar and Northangerland and Gordon, to be yielded up to me unconditionally and immediately in just right to myself and my heirs in due and rightful sovereignty now and hereafter" (*EW* 123).

2 **Lord Charles Albert Florian Wellesley**: younger brother of Zamorna. Although, judging from the way he is treated by adults, he appears to be a child of perhaps nine or ten years (see note 78 below), Charles' sardonic narratorial style seems to reflect an adult sensibility which is often at odds with his putative age. Charlotte engages Charles and her other main narrator, CaptainTree, in an amusing rivalry in the early Angria stories (see, for example, *Albion and Marina* and *The Foundling, ECB*).

3 **The Children ... departed:** This paragraph is a patchwork of Biblical quotations. "The Children ... amongst us": cf. Exodus 7:5, 12:41, I John 2:19; "mixed ... *cattle*": Exodus 12:37-38; "Baal-Zephon ... Zin": Exodus 14:2, 16:1; "A pillar ... by day": Exodus 13:21-22 (note reversal of day and night); "spoiled the Egyptians": Exodus 12:36; "not slain our first-born": Exodus 12:29; "cast ... us": Proverbs 1:14; "Ichabod ... departed!": I Samuel 4:21. On the use of Biblical language in *My Angria* generally, see the appendix on "'The Best Book' and This Book." ("Cf." preceding a Biblical reference denotes an inexact quotation or an echo of the Biblical text.)

4 **King Adrian**: Arthur Augustus Adrian Wellesley, King of Angria, Duke of Zamorna, Marquis of Douro. Arthur Wellesley, usually known as Zamorna, first appears as one of the sons of the Duke of Wellington in *Tales of the Islanders* (1829, *ECB* I.25). He is a minor figure in early stories, but gradually comes to supplant the Duke of Wellington as Charlotte's main focus in the Angrian saga. Zamorna is perhaps the most complex product of Charlotte's taste in literary and historical figures. He is, to varying degrees, part godlike Apollo figure (his emblem is the rising sun), part Sir Walter Scott romantic hero, and part Miltonic Satan (*ECB* II.ii.xv, xvi). Above all, Zamorna reflects Charlotte's fascination, some might even say obsession, with the darker, more tormented aspects of the Byronic hero. This is particularly reflected in his relationships with women. Elsewhere Lord Charles describes Zamorna: "All here is passion and fire unquenchable. Impetuous sin, stormy pride, diving and soaring enthusiasm, war and poetry, are kindling their fires in all his veins, and his wild blood boils from his heart and back again in a torrent of new-sprung lava" (*ECB* II.ii.93).

5 **Verdopolis:** "Verreopolis means the Glass Town, being compounded of a Greek and French word to that effect," says the narrator of *Visits in Verreopolis* (*ECB* I.298). Within the same story the spelling changes to Verdopolis and remains consistent thenceforth. CA suggests that Glass Town has become so sophisticated "by the end of 1830 that even its name must be changed to a more elevated form" (*EW* 59). Descriptions of Verdopolis differ depending upon the moods of the various speakers. The narrator in *The Bridal* (August 20, 1832) comments on "the melancholy solitude of the vast streets and mighty commercial marts of our great Babel; ... the glory, the power, the riches, dominion and radiant beauty of the city which sitteth like a queen upon the waters" (*ECB* I.338). A different perspective comes from Edward Sydney, who exclaims: "And that is Verdopolis! that splendid city rising with such graceful haughtiness from the green realm of Neptune," as he gazes on the city's "proud enduring towers.... Far above him the city walls and ramparts rose to a tremendous height, frowning terribly on the foam-white waves which rushed roaring to their feet. A mingled noise of by-passing multitudes, rolling chariots and tramping horses soared dull and deep over the black battlements" (*The Foundling, ECB* II.i.50-51).

6 **Oriental Noble:** The discourse of orientalism — with its connotations of the exotic, the romantic, the extravagant, and the opulent — is everywhere apparent in *My Angria*. See Introduction.

7 **Glass-Towner:** Charlotte's (and Branwell's) earliest stories take place in the Glass Town Confederacy. In *A Romantic Tale* (April 15, 1829), the Twelve Adventurers, after battling many storms, land on the shore of "Ashantee." They win a battle with its indigenous peoples, and "immediately after the treaty of peace was concluded" they set about building a city: "The situation was in the middle of a large plain, bounded on the north by high mountains, on the south by the sea, on the east by gloomy forests, and on the west by evil deserts" (*ECB* I.11). In the preface to *The Search After Happiness* (August 17, 1829), this town is referred to as "the Glass Town." CA notes Branwell's elaboration in his *The History of the Young Men*: "He ostentatiously quotes 'the Author of the *Romantic Tale*' as an authority for his own history and illustrates his work with a detailed folding map, plotting major cities, roads, rivers and mountain ranges. His map is coloured and labelled according to the various kingdoms founded by the children's four chief characters: Wellington's Land, Parry's Land, Ross's Land and Sneaky's Land. The Great Glass Town is the centre of this confederation of states. Each state has its own particular Glass Town modelled on the capital" (*EW* 32). Charlotte conforms to this reorganization.

8 **half sovereign in shillings and pence:** In nineteenth-century English currency, a sovereign was the coin for one pound, or twenty shillings, each shilling being worth twelve pence. If the "low-born rascallions" could finance the journey to Adrianopolis with ten shillings, the "high-born scoundrels" would spend considerably more.

9 **adventurer's fob:** Johnson defines "fob" as "a small pocket" and provides a quotation from Swift's *Gulliver's Travels* which gives clues to the modern reader as to the location of "fobs" on men's clothing: "There were two pockets which we could not enter; these were called his *fobs*: they were two large slits out into the top of his middle cover, but squeezed close by the pressure of his belly."

10 **filthy lucre:** I Timothy 3:3

11 **noble Niger:** "Named after the original river, the River Niger flows south-east from Sneakiesland to the Great Bay of Glass Town. It separates at Freetown into two, the rivers Niger and Guadima, both of which flow through Verdopolis. Later, the Niger becomes the border between Angria and the old Verdopolitan Federation" (*ECB* II.i.150 n.53). In Verdopolis, the Niger flows past Wellesley House, earlier home of Arthur Wellesley and Mary Henrietta Percy. In the Valley of Verdopolis "the wide, bright billows of the Niger roll through banks that look down in magnificent serenity on their own tree-dropped verdure, sloping into the illimitable depths of skies like oceans, skirted with fertile shores, crossed with the rippling river waves, clouded with vanishing foam as pure and transient as snow-wreaths" (*The Spell*, *ECB* II.i.212).

12 **Guadiama:** The Guadiama (also spelled Guadima) surrounds the city of Verdopolis before reaching the Great Bay of Glass Town. It flows near Waterloo Palace, the residence of the Duke of Wellington in Verdopolis. The river receives a line in "A National Ode for the Angrians": "Guadima rolls exultingly with sunshine on its breast" (*PCB* 172).

13 **Adrianopolis:** Named after Arthur Augustus Adrian, King of Angria and Duke of Zamorna, Adrianopolis is the capital of the eastern Kingdom of Angria. Branwell describes "the great inhabited street of the Calabar, whose finished buildings, all resembling rather palaces than houses, and the noble shops blazing on each hand of us, with the thickly-peopled state of the promenade and the air of life and bustle which seemed to reign through this thoroughfare of an almost unborn City" (*MUW* I.437).

14 **Calabar:** Adrianopolis is on the banks of the Calabar, which is named after the real river in West Africa. On November 17, 1837 Charlotte wrote:

> The Calabar! The Calabar!
> The sacred land it laves,
> I little thought, so lone, so far
> To hear its rolling waves.
>
> To see and hear them in their course
> As clear, as they who stand
> And watch the unbridled torrent force
> Its way through Angria's land. (*PCB* 215)

15 **Babylon:** the magnificent ancient city famous for its wealth and luxury. Verdopolis is "often referred to as the Babylon of Africa" (*ECB* II.i.134).

16 **Sydneyan, a St Dairian or an Ardrahian passion**: Edward Sydney was formerly an ally of Zamorna (see *The Foundling*), but he has now joined Arthur, Marquis of Ardrah, and other Verdopolitan politicians in strongly opposing Zamorna's decision to form a new kingdom of Angria. Ardrah voices his unhappiness with Zamorna in *The Scrap Book*. The source of St Dairian is unclear.

17 **shog:** In Scots and/or East Yorkshire dialect this means to proceed at a leisurely but steady pace, jog along, keep going.

18 **Honorable Julia, Lady Sydney:** A prominent Verdopolitan, she is married to Edward Sydney, and is also cousin to Zamorna.

19 **Lady Maria Percy:** not to be confused with Mary Henrietta Percy. In yet another example of the Angrians' tortuously complex familial relationships, Lady Maria is the former Princess Maria Sneachie, who has recently married Edward Percy, disinherited son of Alexander Percy.

20 **Crack of Doom:** refers to the heralding of the Biblical apocalypse in the Book of John, to the "last trump, the signal for the final judgement" (*Brewer's*).

21 **Lady N —:** Julia is referring to Zenobia, wife to Alexander Percy, Lord Northangerland. Lord Charles writes of her "unbridled excess of passion … the fire in her eye and command on her brow," and calls her "the prima donna of the Angrian Court, the most learned woman of her age, the modern Cleopatra, the Verdopolitan de Stael: in a word, Zenobia Percy!" (*ECB* II.ii.88). Although married, Zenobia, like most women, is captivated by Zamorna's fatal charm. One of Charlotte's other narrators, Captain Tree, even suggests that Percy nearly kills Zenobia in a fit of jealousy over Zamorna (see *The Foundling*), but later this charge is angrily refuted by Charles Wellesley.

22 **Great Angrian Premier**: Alexander Percy, Lord Northangerland. Like Mary Henrietta, Alexander Percy was first created by Branwell Brontë. Known as "the Rogue" in his initial incarnation, he was a pirate and ne'er-do-well. Charlotte first makes significant use of him in *The Green Dwarf, a Tale of the Perfect Tense*. In this and other Angrian stories, Charlotte transforms Percy the pirate into Percy the powerful political figure with a dark past, and she intertwines his fortunes with those of Zamorna. Zamorna marries Percy's daughter, Mary Henrietta, and makes Percy the prime minister of his newly formed kingdom of Angria, but, as we see in *My Angria and the Angrians*, this tenuous alliance has (at least temporarily) broken down.

23 **York Place:** residence of Lady Julia Wellesley and Edward Sydney in the city of Verdopolis.

24 ***My* Edward**: Edward Sydney, Lady Julia's husband, as opposed to Lady Maria's husband, Edward Percy. Julia is contrasting Maria's newly-wedded happiness to her own marriage, which has turned sour after the promising beginning recounted by Charlotte in *The Foundling*.

25 **lives ... has his being:** Acts 17:28. Lady Sydney's sarcasm is sharpened by the allusion, since Paul's point in Acts is that men live, move, and have their being in God (and certainly not in politics).

26 **Our uprising and our down-lying:** Cf. Psalms 139:2.

27 **My country ... etc.:** Although CB would have had no opportunity to witness personally Parliamentary theatrics of the type parodied here, she had certainly read many accounts of them. Speeches were widely reported in the periodical press of which the Brontës were such avid consumers (see Introduction). This passage indicates a rather irreverant attitude to political oratory.

28 **dernier ressort:** French for "last resort." The taste fashionable society had for incorporating French phrases into everyday speech is humorously mocked in Frances Burney's *Cecilia* (1782), among other works. Notably, French phrases and dialogue would come to punctuate much of the mature work of CB, probably the result of her long visit to Brussels between 1842-44. See *Jane Eyre* and *Villette*.

29 **diamond ... plumes:** A bandeau is a "narrow band or fillet worn by women to bind the hair, or as part of a headdress" (*OED*). Sir William Beechey's 1831 protrait of Queen Alexandra depicts her with a pearl bandeau as part of her elaborately pinned and stiffened coiffure (see Foster 51). Large feathers were fashionable trimmings for hats, hairstyles, and bonnets in the late 1820s and early 1830s (Cunnington 396). Note also that it is the "ancient countesses" who are so richly adorned; as fashion historians C. Willett and Phillis Cunnington have written, "it was becoming correct [in the 1830s] for the unmarried young woman to wear little more jewellery than a neck chain and bracelets with evening dress; the matron however was much more resplendent" (419).

30 **Castlereagh ... Arundel ... Edward Percy ... Northangerland ... Thornton**: Many of Charlotte's characters are based on real persons. Castlereagh, for instance, is named after Viscount Robert Stewart Castlereagh, a former British Foreign Secretary who met with an unfortunate end. Castlereagh

was blackmailed after being "enticed into a brothel by what turned out to be a young man in women's clothing" and committed suicide in 1822 (Thompson 38). The name Arundel comes from the Earldom of Arundel, which, according to *Debrett's Peerage*, was first established in 1138. Arundel Castle is located in Sussex. Edward Percy is the son of Alexander Percy, Lord Northangerland, the new Premier of Angria. Northangerland is, of course, Alexander Percy (see also note 22). Thornton is probably General Wilson Thornton, Charles Wellesley's guardian.

31 **old Trojans:** *Brewer's* notes that the Trojans in Homer's *Iliad* and Virgil's *Aeneid* are described as truthful, brave, patriotic and confiding.

32 **Countess Zenobia**: Lady Northangerland. See also note 21.

33 **keen:** an adjective of which CB was uncommonly fond. She often uses it, as in this instance, to describe a penetrating gaze. However, in keeping with her heightened sensitivity, she frequently uses the word to describe intense or passionate feelings or the piercing of the soul by the elemental world, as is often the case in *Villette*.

34 **Mary Percy:** Mary Henrietta Percy. Daughter of Alexander Percy, Lord Ellrington/Northangerland, and third wife of Arthur Wellesley, Mary Henrietta is first introduced into the Angrian saga by Branwell Brontë, in *The Politics of Verdopolis* (November 1833). In January 1834, Charlotte takes up Mary Henrietta's character in *A Leaf in an Unopened Volume*, and she occupies a fairly prominent place in subsequent instalments as the often unhappy pawn of Zamorna and Northangerland, the two dominant and frequently conflicting personalities of the Angria series.

35 **felo de se:** an Anglo-Latin expression that refers both to the act of suicide, and the self-murderer.

36 **sue for a separate maintenance:** marital separation. At this time in the nineteenth century, divorces were expensive, scandalous, and extremely difficult to achieve, particularly for women. However, in situations of incompatibility, couples could contrive to live apart; this often took the form of an allowance — a separate maintenance — of funds and property for the wife, whose own assets had become her husband's at the time of their marriage.

37 **Eastern Paradise:** refers to Adrianopolis. The phrase is also yet another echo of the orientalism so prevalent in the text.

38 **Reader:** an early instance of CB's charming habit of engaging her audience in terms of an individual reader. The most famous example, and one of English literature's more provocative instances of meiosis, occurs at the conclusion of *Jane Eyre* when Jane remarks simply, "Reader, I married him."

39 **Charles Wellesley**: Our narrator here refers to himself in the third person.

40 **Girnington Hall:** The country residence of General Thornton, and therefore, by extension, residence of Lord Charles Wellesley, Thornton's ward.

41 **nakedness of the land:** Genesis 42:9; cf. Numbers 13:16 et seq.

42 **evening of the sixth day:** Genesis 1:31

43 **chance of a cast:** The modern equivalent of CB's colloquial use of "cast" here is "hitch" — i.e. one might "hitch a ride." See *OED*.

44 **Castle of Giant Despair:** In the first part of Bunyan's *Pilgrim's Progress* (1678), Doubting Castle is the place where the giant Despair and his wife Diffidence live, and where Christian and Hopeful are imprisoned until they secure a key called Promise.

45 **Edwardston Hall:** Edward Percy's country seat near Verdopolis.

46 **Sydenham Hills:** The Sydenham Hills, as in this instance, are often distinguished by their colour. For example, in "A National Ode for the Angrians": "The ancient hills of Sydenham have never felt the glow / Of such a dawn as that which burns their blushing summits now" (*PCB* 172); and in *Caroline Vernon* (1839), CB writes: "the remoter hills of the same range rolled away clad in dusky woodland — till distance softened them & the summer sky embued them with intense violet" (*Five Novelettes* 288).

47 **The horizon ... heaven:** This passage, in its subject matter and colourful use of language, anticipates the vivid landscape descriptions of *Jane Eyre* and is perhaps also reflective of CB's lifelong interest in the visual arts.

48 **little black ratan:** The *OED* defines rattan (ratan) as a "switch or stick of rattan, used for beating a person or thing, or for carrying in the hand." This adds a rather ominous note to the caricature of Branwell. Rattan was grown principally in the East Indies; its easy availability is one more manifestation of the widespread benefits of Britain's imperial reach at this time.

49 **Wiggins:** a caricature of Branwell Brontë (1817-1848). Charlotte first introduces the character in the earlier Angrian tale "A Day Abroad," part of *Corner Dishes* (see *ECB* II.ii.109); he distinguishes himself in that episode by remarking, and then laying hands, on the incredible nose of Mary Percy. Here, the figure of Wiggins captures Branwell's extravagant imagination and ambition, his dreams to succeed at everything, but his inability to commit seriously to anything. At seventeen, Branwell aspired to be a painter, a musician, a boxer, and a man of distinction — as well as a co-writer of the Angrian stories — but as the events of his later life proved, social awkwardness and extreme self-doubt prevented him from realizing any of these great expectations held by his family or himself.

50 **Zamorna**: a city in the recently formed kingdom of Angria. It is a sign of Arthur Wellesley's preeminence that both the city and the province in which it is located are named after him.

51 **Mr Greenwood**: music instructor for many high-ranking Verdopolians, including Mary Henrietta and Zamorna. CA has suggested that Greenwood and other musicians in the Angria stories are based on real musicians of the period (*ECB* II.ii.109 nn.92-93). Greenwood meets with Benjamin Patrick Wiggins again in *Corner Dishes: A Day Abroad*, where they have an unfortunate encounter concerning Mary Henrietta's nose.

52 **first-rate snip:** a colloquial name for a tailor, also employed as an allusive personal name for a tailor (*OED*).

53 **Parsee:** Parsees are descendants of Persians who fled to India in the seventh and eighth centuries to escape Mohammedan persecution on account of their religious practice of Zoroastrianism (*OED*). As John Fryer notes in his 1698 *New Account of East India and Persia*, Zoroastrians "worship the Sun and Adore the Elements."

54 **Juggernaut:** a Hindu God, "Lord of the World," whose festival involves dragging an effigy of the God in a car over the sands of India to another temple. As with other British myths concerning India and its inhabitants at this time, the belief that fanatical pilgrims cast themselves under the wheels of the car to be crushed to death on the last day of the festival is untrue.

55 **bombardones ... ramgalongtonas:** The bombardone was a predecessor of the tuba; also, another name for the ophicleide, which was basically a keyed bugle. *The New Grove Dictionary of Musical Instruments* notes that "there were no less than three ophicleides [and] four serpents" at York in 1835. (This may be the first appearance of "bombardone" in English; the earliest use recorded by the *OED* was in 1856). "Cyclopede," an abbreviation of encyclopedia, has never been the name of a musical instrument (Wiggins's fantastic imagination is in play here, as in the unimaginable "ramgalongtona"). The serpent was "a bass wind instrument of deep tone, made of wood covered with leather and formed with three U-shaped turns" (*OED*); the name comes from its snake-like shape.

56 **Thorncliffe ... Howard:** slightly disguised versions of real locations in the Brontës' world, Thornton and Haworth. Branwell was born at Thornton on June 26, 1817; from 1820, the Brontë family lived at the parsonage in the small town of Haworth, in Yorkshire.

57 **Warner Howard Warner:** Warner is the Prime Minister of Angria, Lord-Lieutenant of the city of Angria, head of one of Angria's oldest families, and an ally to Zamorna. Given Warner's power and influence, it is not surprising that his name is everywhere in Angrian geography (e.g. Howard, Warner Hills, Howard Church).

58 **Free Town:** named after the capital of Sierra Leone on the West African Coast, settled by freed slaves from 1787.

59 **moss-hags:** holes made for the extraction of peat. "Hag" here comes from an Old Norse word meaning "cutting blow," and is etymologically distinct from the familiar homonym.

60 **Sneachie's Glass-Town:** (also spelled Sneaky's Glass Town). "The capital cities of all the kingdoms in the Verdopolitan Federation were named after the original Glass Town, now Verdopolis" (*ECB* II.ii.47 n.79); hence Sneachie's Glass-Town is the capital of Sneachiesland, the northern kingdom of the Verdopolitan Federation.

61 **re-piece-en:** "Re-piece" is to piece two objects which have been separated together again (*OED*).

62 **Charlotte Wiggins, Jane Wiggins and Anne Wiggins:** Branwell's sisters, Charlotte (b. April 21, 1816), Emily Jane (b. July 30, 1818) and Anne Brontë (b. January 17, 1820); at the time *My Angria* was written, in 1834, Charlotte was eighteen, Branwell seventeen, Emily sixteen, and Anne fourteen. While Branwell might have teased his sisters on their appearance, portraits of the family that Branwell painted during this period represent his sisters as healthy and attractive, though not conventionally beautiful.

63 **I wasn't satisfied ... sempstresses:** The Brontë sisters, Charlotte and Anne in particular, were determined to survive in the world economically, but were initially resigned to a life of obscurity as school-teachers or governesses. The whole family unrealistically pinned its hopes for a grand future on Branwell, suggested here by Wiggins' over-the-top visions of fame and fortune. However, while Charlotte looked up to Branwell as the family hero, her sense of humour still allowed her to satirize his ambition and his "toadyism" in the figure of Wiggins.

64 **Bach ... Byron ... Claude Lorrain ... Alexander Rogue ... Edward Percy ... Grenville ... De Humbolt, Ledyard, Mungo Park:** Johannes Sebastian Bach (1685-1750), famous baroque composer. George Gordon, Lord Byron (1788-1824), romantic poet and ladies' man (see notes 87 and 115 below). Claude Lorrain (aka Claude Gellée, 1600-1682), French painter and master of the ideal landscape form. Alexander Rogue (aka Alexander Percy, Lord Northangerland), Edward Percy and Grenville are all fictional characters in the Angrian tales. Alexander, Baron von Humboldt (1769-1859), German naturalist and traveller. John Ledyard (1751-88), American traveller. Mungo Park (1771-1806?), Scottish explorer of the Niger (see also *ECB* II.ii.250 nn.42-44). All of these men, fictional or otherwise, were renowned for their abilities in their respective fields — and Wiggins, with his Branwellian modesty, intends to surpass them all!

65 **Otaheite:** Tahiti.

66 **to heaven in a fiery chariot:** Cf. II Kings 2:11. A fitting culmination to Wiggins's (imagined) career.

67 **Stumpsland:** (also spelled Stump's Land and Stumps's Island): "An island off the African coast south of Wellingtonsland, originally founded by Stumps, one of the Twelves, but now a remote holiday resort for the older members of Verdopolitan society" (*ECB* II.ii.251 n.48).

68 **Mr Sudbury Figgs ... Mr Abey Figgs:** probably an irreverent reference to Abraham Stansfield Sunderland, organist at the Keighley parish church, who was a music teacher. The passage is interesting for its reference to Branwell's musical ambitions, which have been less prominent in portraits of him than his artistic and authorial aspirations (see *MUW* II.2).

69 **"And the Glory ... Redeemer Liveth":** Both pieces are from Handel's oratorio, *The Messiah.*

70 **"this is a god and not a man!":** Acts 12:22. Wiggins usually applies Scripture in a hyperbolic and sacrilegious way.

71 **licking the dust under them:** Cf. Isaiah 49:23.

72 **Black Bull public house:** The Black Bull Hotel, near Haworth Parsonage, was a favourite resort of Branwell Brontë. That "Bull," even in its nineteenth-century applications, means to jest, deceive or make self-contradictory propositions suggests that a pub named the Black Bull is a very appropriate retreat for Branwell and Wiggins alike.

73 **ignis-fatuus:** the descriptive name of a natural phenomenon common in the Yorkshire moors. Literally "foolish fire" (Latin) it is a flame-like phosphorescence that hovers over marshy ground — which arises due to the spontaneous combustion of gases flowing from decaying vegetable matter — and deludes people who attempt to follow it. Here, the expression takes on a more general meaning, and implies any delusive aim or object.

74 **as aimless as the clouds that float a summer heaven upon:** While not a direct or accurate quotation from any poet, this line, as CA notes, captures the spirit of Wordsworth's "I wandered lonely as a cloud" (1807) and says much about the narrator's proclivity for the romantic, as well as CB's enthusiasm for the Romantic poets.

75 **Edward Percy's New Mill:** Percy rises from humble beginnings to become a captain of industry and Angrian Minister of Trade. His factories come to dominate the main towns so that, eventually, Zamorna City becomes "as thriving as any industrial Yorkshire town of the 1830s" (*EW* 177).

76 **Olympia:** One of Angria's rivers, it flows through Zamorna City. The river receives a line in "The National Ode for the Angrians": "Olympia's waves glance clear along their wandering line of blue" (*PCB* 172).

77 **Zamorna Hills:** "Zamorna lifts her fruitful hills like Eden's to the sky, / And fair as Enna's fields of flowers her golden prairies lie" (from "A National Ode for the Angrians," *PCB* 172).

78 **Little villainous imp:** It is as well to remember that our narrator, Lord Charles Wellesley, is at this time only nine years old, by Christine Alexander's computation (*EW* 128). The children in the Brontës' fiction, like the Brontë children themselves, were notably precocious in their command of language. Six-year-old Paulina Home in *Villette*, though minuscule in size, can still articulate her feelings. According to Jane Eyre, as she looks back on her ten-year-old self, "Children can feel, but they cannot analyse their feeling: and if the analysis is partially effected in thought, they know not how to express the result of the process in words" (*JE* ch 3). Charles Wellesley, however, though still a "little ... imp," has a masterly control of language.

79 **Welcome Heroes to the War:** A patriotic Angrian anthem, attributed here to Alexander Soult, Marquis of Marseilles, one of Branwell Brontë's pseudonyms. Marshal Soult was Wellington's opponent in the Peninsular Wars and again at Waterloo, under Napoleon. Branwell also uses the name "Young Soult" as a pseudonym in the early juvenilia. The Marquis of Marseilles later becomes the Angrian Ambassador to Verdopolis and Duke of Dalmatia on the death of his father.

80 **Lady Lieutenant and the Countess of Arundel**: Christine Alexander identifies "Lady Lieutenant" as Harriet, Lady Castlereagh (*ECB* II.ii.80, n. 59). The Countess of Arundel is Edith, the former Princess Royal of Sneachie's Land. She marries Frederic, Viscount Lofty and Earl of Arundel in *High Life in Verdopolis*.

81 **His "gods ... her country":** Ruth 1:16.

82 **Palace of St Mary, the hill of Elimbos, the loch:** landmarks in Sneachiesland.

83 **Genii:** The Brontë children, especially Charlotte and Branwell, were the original "Genii," the gods of this creation who turned Branwell's toy soldiers into the Twelve Adventurers and subsequently directed the "plays."

84 **Angria:** refers to Angria Province. "And Angria calls from mount and vale, from wood and heather-dell, / A song of joy and thankfulness on rushing winds to swell" (from "A National Ode for the Angrians," *PCB* 175). The following is from Branwell's checklist: "ANGRIA. 80 miles long, 180 broad. Capital. The City of Angria. Lord Lieutenant. W.H. Warner, Esq. Population. 1,492,000" (*EW* 125).

85 **drawing it mild:** "Draw it mild" is a common English expression analogous to "Don't exaggerate." The allusion is to "drawing" ale.

86 **"Sound the loud trumpets ...":** The anthem opens with typical Angrian grandeur:

> Sound the loud trumpets o'er Afric's sea;
> Zamorna hath triumphed; the Angrians are free.
> Sound, for our day Star hath risen in glory;
> Sound that loud Trumpet, unequalled in story. (*MUW* I.435)

87 **many a bright eye lingered on his form:** One of Zamorna's Byronic qualities is his fatal attractiveness to women. Zamorna's past is littered with numerous affairs and at least three marriages; in *A Late Occurrence* he even has a group of female adherents, "twenty-two noble girls" who all wear "black satin and scarlet flowers" in his honour (*EW* 117-120).

88 **Circassian foot:** The Circassians, one of the peoples living in the north Caucasus region, were widely renowned for their attractiveness; e.g. Edmund Spencer, writing in the 1830's, celebrates their "beauty of feature and symmetry of form," and adds, "some of the finest statues of the ancients do not display, in their productions, greater perfection" (206-7). Circassian women, in particular, were known for the "delicate smallness" of their hands and feet (cf. Spencer 206).

89 **there's no faith in complexion:** Lady Castlereagh is correct in recognizing these as false whiskers, an assumed disguise. The Brontës were strong believers in "complexion" and physiognomy as reliable guides to character, and as difficult to be concealed. The penetrating of this disguise looks forward to Jane Eyre's recognition of Rochester in his gipsy fortune-teller's guise. "I at once noticed that hand. It was no more the withered limb of eld than my own: it was a rounded supple member ..." (*JE* ch 19).

90 **Two primer cracks:** In Scots dialect, a "crack" is an individual who has a talent for conversation; it is also an antiquated English term for a lively lad, a wag (*OED*).

91 **rattons:** CA suggests that CB is referring to 'rats' in Scots dialect.

92 **Adrians:** the new Angrian currency, named after Zamorna.

93 **Was she thinking of Sydney?**: her husband, Edward Sydney. Julia later leaves Sydney and marries General Wilson Thornton, Charles Wellesley's guardian.

94 **She cannot be a guest at my brother's house**: Cecillia Seymour has recently married William Percy (see *The Spell*), who is quarreling with his brother, Edward. At this point, the exact nature of their disagreement isn't clear, although it probably concerns William's quitting the sheep business in favour of a military life.

95 **Elm Grove Villa:** On her first sight of Elm Grove Villa, Lily Hart "beheld one of the fairest and most fertile scenes imagination can conceive. Emerald-green meadows stretched on every side, spotted here and there with tall, spreading forest trees and watered by a broad and placid river on whose banks, facing the east and bathed in the rosy light of early day, there appeared a small and elegant villa surrounded by a lawn and gardens" (*ECB* II.i.311).

96 **Georgiana and Eliza:** Compare Eliza and Georgiana Reed, Jane Eyre's cousins. While Eliza is "tall … thin … sallow," Georgiana shares some features with this earlier pair of siblings. To match their "yellow hair, snowy skins and haughty blue eyes," she has "yellow hair" and "languishing blue eyes," and she is "fair as waxwork" (*JE* ch 19).

97 **Cecillia, fairy … fingers:** The magisterial calling for music recalls Mr Rochester, who accuses Jane of being a mischief-making fairy, and commands her, "Sit down at the piano and play a song" (*JE* ch 13).

98 **Conqueror mail coach:** Thomas De Quincey recalls in "The English Mail Coach" (1849) his days of riding on mail coaches, and he refers to the nationalist zeal with which mail coaches were greeted by the citizenry during the Napoleonic Wars, since they often carried news of England's martial victories. CB may have something of this sort in mind when she places the Angrian nobility in a mail coach called the Conqueror.

99 **scarlet roquelaure:** a man's cloak of the eighteenth and early nineteenth centuries, named after the Duke of Roquelaure (1656-1738), which reached to the knee. The villainous Marquis de Montalt wears a roquelaure while in pursuit of the virtuous Adeline in Mrs Radcliffe's gothic novel *The Romance of the Forest* (1791): "Presently he saw a gentleman, wrapped up in a roquelaure, alight and enter the inn" (Vol II, ch. 11).

100 **gas-lit:** Gas lighting was first installed in Pall Mall in London in 1807 and, in the decades after the granting of the first charter to the Gas Light and Coke Company in 1812, gradually replaced "the feeble flicker of the old oil-lamps and their foul smell" (Margetson 126). This far-off African colony is thus admirably modern in its early adoption of gas lighting.

101 **wynd:** in Scots dialect, a narrow, frequently winding street or lane leading off a main thoroughfare in a town.

102 **Saul-like figure:** The Biblical chronicler says of Saul: "[T]here was not among the children of Israel a goodlier person than he: from his shoulders and upward he was higher than any of the people" (I Samuel 9:2).

103 **the Homer and the Maecenas of his age:** Maecenas (?-8 B.C.) was a friend of Augustus and the patron of Horace, Virgil, and Propertius. The phrase suggests that Zamorna was the ideal combination of poet and patron.

104 **"Arise":** Apparently this is a password which identifies Howard/ Zamorna.

105 **A fine starry night:** This brief exchange between Zamorna and his soldiers, when he addresses them personally, suggests a reminiscence of Shakespeare's warrior king Henry V, when he provides "A little touch of Harry in the night" (*Henry V* IV chorus 45).

106 **penetralia:** the innermost parts or recesses of a building (*OED*).

107 **clear, large star of beauty:** This vision of almost supernatural feminine beauty as connected with heavenly bodies recurs in CB's writings. In *The Twelve Adventurers*, written at 13, she envisioned a female deity emanating from the moon and stars to quell the turbulent "Genius of the Storm" (*Twelve Adventurers* 10-12). Jane Eyre's painting of the serene "Evening Star" shows "the dim forehead ... crowned with a star" (*JE* ch 13). And Jane receives supernatural guidance from a lunar deity: "She broke forth as never moon yet burst from cloud ... inclining a glorious brow earthward" (ch 27). All these figures, like Queen Mary Henrietta, are touched with a certain solemn melancholy as well as with authority.

108 **a priceless pearl ... strong man:** a conflation of Matthew 13:46 and Mark 3:27.

109 **One word ... Mary:** Cf. John 20:15, 16. See the appendix on "'The Best Book' and This Book."

110 **of earth, earthy:** I Corinthians 15:47.

111 **messenger of Satan:** II Corinthians 12:7.

112 **dust in the balance:** Isaiah 40:15.

113 **eat the bread ... in safety?:** "Eat the bread and drink the waters of bitterness" is a vaguely Biblical phrase. Possible sources are I Kings 22:27 and Revelation 8:11. For "the light of your countenance," cf. Psalms 4:6, 89:15; for "sleep in peace and awake in safety," cf. Psalms 34:8.

114 **Philippa ... Esther:** The intercession of Philippa (c.1314-1369), Edward III's French consort, saved the burghers of Calais from his wrath after he besieged and took the town in 1347. Esther, a Jewess, successfully pleaded with her husband, King Ahasuerus of Persia, to reverse his orders for the extermination of her people. See the book of Esther, especially 7:2-5 and 8:2-6.

115 **That tinge of insanity:** a reference to Zamorna's unstable Byronic nature. Charlotte, like many young women, was fascinated by the Byronic hero's dark, sensual, dangerous, and slightly evil personality; Lady Caroline Lamb, one of Byron's lovers, summed up his unique appeal by calling him "mad, bad and dangerous to know." Inappropriate as Byron might have been as a role model for a parson's young daughter, the Romantic figure came to exert a tremendous influence on her nevertheless. Echoes of the Byronic character make themselves felt in Charlotte's later fictional heroes, especially Rochester, the disturbed and brooding love interest in *Jane Eyre* (interestingly, Rochester is spared Zamorna's madness, but the ill-fated Bertha is not). The glamourized insanity that Zamorna exhibits here has somewhat uncertain origins in fact; Byron's wife, Annabella Milbanke, certainly believed, and tried to prove, that Byron was mad but whether he actually was is subject to some debate. In his last period of illness, he did experience signs of acute anxiety, as well as seizures, both of which made him fear for his own mental health.

116 **fierce dilated zones:** This seems to be a uniquely Brontëan expression. The *OED* has no mention of the word "zones" referring specifically to "eyes"; however, a zone can be defined as "a part of the surface of a sphere contained between two parallel planes." CB may be stretching this geometrical term to describe the visible portion of Zamorna's glaring eyes.

117 **Duke of Wellington**: Charles's and Zamorna's father, patterned after the famous military hero. Charlotte initially envisioned him as the central figure in her stories, calling him "my chief man" in early collaborations with Branwell (*Tales of the Islanders*, June 30, 1829). He is gradually supplanted, however, as Charlotte's interest shifts toward his son, Arthur Wellesley.

118 **Lady Victorine**: Lady Helen Victorine Gordon, Zamorna's first wife.

119 **The organs of vision ... glazed:** Zamorna's seizure and temporary blindness link him not only with Byron (see note 115), but also with certain blind poets and seers such as Homer, Tiresias, and Milton, whose physical blindness allowed for visions "Of things invisible to mortal sight" (*Paradise Lost*, III.55).

120 **I shall wear you out soon — as I did — Hem!**: Zamorna is alluding to the unfortunate death of his first wife, Lady Helen Victorine Gordon. Zamorna is notoriously hard on wives, having buried two others (Lady Helen and Florence Marian Hume) before marrying Mary Henrietta.

121 **Sir Copley Lyndhurst:** named after John Singleton Copley, Lord Lyndhurst (1772-1863), son of the famous American painter of the same name, and Lord Chancellor of England throughout all the Tory governments from 1827 to 1846, including Wellington's term as prime minister.

122 **Old Doit:** According to *Brewer's*, "doit" is an old Dutch coin of low value; hence, anything of little worth, a trifle.

123 **I should be wae ... for his sake:** CA suggests that Zamorna echoes (or attempts to quote from) Burns' *Address to the Deil*: "I'm wae to think

upo' yon den,/Ev'n for your sake"; here "wae" means "grieved" or "sorry."

124 **one of the Twelves:** The original Twelve Adventurers who founded Glass Town did not include Badhi, but he appears in early manuscripts. His death and substantial legacy are of convenience to Zamorna.

125 **most worthy crocodiles:** Zamorna implies that any tears shed for this death would be "crocodile tears," or hypocritical ones. The crocodile was said to mourn over even its prey. "The mournful crocodile / With sorrow snares relenting passengers" (Shakespeare, *2 Henry VI* III.i.226-7). It is Zamorna's flight of fancy to throw in "alligators."

126 **Paganini's fiddle:** Nicolo Paganini (1782-1840), violin virtuoso whose considerable celebrity was owing to both musical talent and scandalous living. To gossip about Paganini was very fashionable. He gave a series of concerts in London in 1833 and 1834, during which time he became the subject of scandal owing to his love affair with a woman much younger than himself.

127 **corners of the mouth ... suffusion of bile:** CB and her siblings were well read in the conventions of facial expressions and their physiological origins, as explained by Charles Le Brun in *A Method to Learn to Design the Passions* (trans. 1734) and by his followers. Black and yellow bile were associated with melancholy, and were said to produce a "yellow" or "ochrey" complexion.

128 **rose of Sharon ... the valley!:** an ironic allusion to the description of the ideal lover in the Song of Solomon 2:1.

129 **My dear William ... my Patroclus:** As CA notes, Zamorna invokes classical and biblical models of ideal friendship between men; notably, by identifying William in the subject positions that follow his name, Zamorna implicitly adopts the roles of the more significant, heroic figures (i.e. David, Damon, Orestes, Aeneas, Achilles). Jonathan was David's closest friend (I Samuel 18:1-4), and Joab was David's advisor and the commander of his army (II Samuel 8:16 and I Chronicles 27:34).

130 **non compos mentis:** from the Latin, "not master of one's right mind" (*OED*).

131 **The next epistle must be an autograph:** It is tactful of Zamorna to decide to write this letter himself, instead of dictating it as he did the last, since this letter is to his mistress, and his wife is present.

132 **Mornington Court:** "Zamorna's ancestral home in Wellingtonsland; the real Duke of Wellington's grandfather was the first Lord Mornington, a title that passed to Wellington's father and eldest brother" (*ECB* II.ii.113 n.103).

133 **Wellingtonstown:** Presumably Wellington's Glass Town, capital city of the Wellingtonsland kingdom of the Verdopolitan Federation.

134 **build you a little fairy pavillion:** CB's men like to be fanciful in imagining residences for the ladies they incline to. Mr Rochester tells the child Adèle that he will take his fairy bride "to the moon, and there I shall

seek a cave in one of the white valleys among the volcano-tops, and mademoiselle shall live with me there" (*JE* ch 24).

135 **Hawkscliffe Forest:** "Zamorna's Angrian estate, at the foot of the Sydenham Hills in the province of Angria" (*ECB* II.ii.278 n.109). It also merits a line in "A National Ode for the Angrians": "And Hawkscliffe's bright and bowery glades uplift their matin hymn" (*PCB* 172).

136 **bonny:** In Scots dialect, this means "beautiful" or "pretty." CA notes that this phrase is actually from the Scottish air subsequently identified by Augustus, which was written by Robert Tannahill. A transcribed copy of this song still survives in Branwell Brontë's book of music for the flute, and there is much to suggest that the other Brontës were especially fond of this kind of music.

137 **my Alexander's portrait ... vivified:** The motif of the portrait that comes alive, familiar in Gothic novels, is prominent even in CB's "realistic" novels. In *Villette* (1853) Lucy Snowe is bewildered when a portrait seems to be replaced by a real person: "The picture seemed to give way. ... Distincter even than these scenic details stood the chief figure — Cunegonde, the sorceress!" (*V* ch 34).

138 **Alpha:** Cf. Revelation 1:11; "Alpha" and "Zenobia" are a play on alpha and omega, the first and last letters of the Greek alphabet.

139 **fear nothing, I am with you:** Genesis 26:24, Matthew 18:20.

140 **We must ... vowed:** Ecclesiastes 5:4.

141 **some lines of lyrical poetry:** This poem, with its predilection for graves, corpses, romance, and extravagant emotionalism, recalls in both style and subject matter such popular writers as L.E.L. (Letitia Elizabeth Landon). *The Venetian Bracelet* (1829), for example, closes with a view of a "lonely tomb, / Hid in the darkness of a cloister's gloom" over which stoops a female "figure closely veil'd" (49-50). Compare also the following lines from *The Improvisatrice* (1824): "A cold white statue; as the blood stood / Had, when in vain her last wild prayer, / Flown to her heart, and frozen there. / ... A funeral pall — her long black hair / Fell over her; herself the tomb / Of her own youth, and breath, and bloom" (quoted by Greer 276).

142 **hast thou ... sphere?:** An echo of Wordsworth's lyric of 1800, "A Slumber Did My Spirit Seal":

> A slumber did my spirit seal;...
> No motion has she now, no force;
> She neither hears nor sees;
> Rolled round in earth's diurnal course,
> With rocks, and stones, and trees. (ll. 1, 5-8)

143 **behold/The Face ... infold:** This gothic touch anticipates Heathcliff's ghoulish visit to Catherine's grave, some sixteen years after her death, to open her coffin: "I saw her face again — it is still hers!" (*WH* ch. 29).

144 **cere-cloth:** "cloth smeared over with glutinous matter" (*Johnson's Dictionary*, 1755); "a waxed winding sheet [for a corpse]" (*OED*).

145 **the pitcher ... shivered:** Ecclesiastes 12:6.

146 **St Abdiel ... St Cyprian:** St Abdiel is named for the faithful angel who opposes Satan's plans to revolt in *Paradise Lost* (V, 803-906). Milton took the name from I Chronicles 5:15. St Cyprian is named for Thascius Caecilius Cyprianus (c. 200-258), Christian martyr and a father of the Church. Anglican and Catholic churches are often named after saints, and angels can be given that title in honour of their holiness ("saint" from Latin "sanctus," meaning sacred, holy). The church at Haworth, for example, is called St Michael and All Angels.

147 **unto us a child is born:** Isaiah 9:6.

148 **could find ... foot.:** Genesis 8:9.

149 **the Duke of Zamorna's other children:** In addition to "the present pair of whelps," Zamorna has two other legitimate children (and there are suggestions of at least one "natural" child). Ernest Edward "Fitzarthur" Wellesley and Arthur Julius Wellesley are the sons of Zamorna's first two wives, Lady Helen Victorine and Marian Hume, respectively. His present wife, Mary Henrietta, goes on to bear him two more children, Arthur and Maria Wellesley (see family tree, page 21).

150 **Wellington's Land:** also Wellingtonsland, western kingdom of the Verdopolitan Federation.

151 **Godfathers ... Godmothers:** The baptismal service in the Book of Common Prayer requires two godfathers and one godmother for each male child; the Angrians, with their usual exuberance, have doubled the number.

152 **that same unknown**: Captain Henry Hastings. According to CA, Hastings "appears in Branwell Brontë's manuscripts at this time and becomes his pseudonym in the later juvenilia" (*ECB* II.ii..288 n.126). Like Patrick Benjamin Wiggins, Hastings also functions as a Branwellesque presence in several of Charlotte's stories, but where Wiggins is a comic satire on Branwell's pretensions, Hastings is more reflective of Branwell's dark and dissolute side.

153 **Hurrah for the Gemini:** This song also appears in *The Spell*. Gemini, Latin for "twins," is a constellation in the Zodiac, and refers to the mythical brothers Castor and Pollux (see *The Spell*, *ECB* II.ii. n.105).

154 **"Lord, now lettest thou ... salvation.":** Luke 2:29-30, the opening phrases of the "Nunc Dimittis," which is part of the Anglican service of Evening Prayer rather than the baptismal service.

155 **vow of renunciation and adoption:** On behalf of the child, sponsors renounce "the devil and all his works, the vain pomp and glory of the world, with all covetous desires of the same, and the carnal desires of the flesh." The baptismal service in the Book of Common Prayer has no vow of adoption. The vow of renunciation comes before the actual baptism; there are a number of discrepancies between the Angrian service and that in the Book of Common Prayer.

156 **"We praise Thee O God! ...":** The opening phrases of the "Te Deum Laudamus," an ancient hymn which is part of the Anglican service of Morning Prayer.

157 **ostrich plumes:** Ostrich plumes on the head were obligatory court wear for women in Great Britain at this time (Cunnington 390).

158 **"in stature ... sons of men":** untraced

159 **in stretching ... insensibility.:** CB makes free and creative use of Acts 20:7-12, in which a young man falls out of a window while St. Paul is preaching. The Biblical account ends: "And they brought the young man alive, and were not a little comforted."

"THE BEST BOOK" AND THIS BOOK

When his children were young, the Rev. Patrick Brontë, "thinking that [they] knew more than I had yet discovered," had each one stand behind a mask and answer a question or two. He asked Charlotte, aged seven, what the best book in the world was? She answered unhesitatingly, "The Bible" (Gaskell 94). It is not surprising, then, to find so many biblical quotations and allusions in *My Angria and the Angrians*. But it is of interest to see how she was weaving this strand of her wide-ranging reading into her fiction.

My Angria opens with a burst of biblical phrases. Quotations from and allusions to "the best book" make up nearly 60% of the words in the first paragraph (81 of 139). Most are drawn from the story of the Exodus — the children of Israel's departure from Egypt:

> The Children of Israel are gone up from amongst us, and a mixed multitude went up with them, and flocks and herds and very much *cattle*. They went by way of Baal-Zephon and are camped in the wilderness of *Sin* (I believe the original orthography is Zin, but that signifies little). A pillar of a cloud went before them, a pillar of cloud by night and of fire by day (is not that the just description of King Adrian, Angrians?) and in their departure they spoiled the Egyptians: they have not slain our first-born, but they enticed them away, saying, cast in your lot with us and we will do you good. Hallelujah should now be the watchword throughout Verdopolis, but alas, some there be who scruple not to cry "Ichabod, Ichabod, the glory is departed!"

The parallels between the two migrations are, of course, ironic. The precocious narrator, Charles Wellesley, adopts the point of view of one of the Egyptians left behind, and selects those details from the biblical account which can either convey his scorn directly or suggest discrepancies between the Old Testament nation and the modern one. The italicizing of "cattle" conveys simple scorn, for example, while the "Children of Israel" clause suggests the mock-heroic character of the Angrian migration, especially with the immediate addition of camp-followers and three contemptuous phrases for the amount of stuff they drag along with them. The pillars of cloud and fire make a similarly ironic comparison.

Not all of the allusions are drawn from the Exodus. "Ichabod, Ichabod, the glory is departed" (I Samuel 4:21) comes later in Israel's history. At the end of a series of episodes emphasising the nation's disobedience, disaster strikes: they are defeated in battle, the Philistines capture the ark of the covenant, the high priest dies, and his two sons are killed. The wife of one of the sons dies too, after bearing a child. Her last words are "The glory is departed from Israel," and she names the child Ichabod (marginal translation, "Where is the glory?"). It is a vivid story, and well used. The Angrians are recast as Philistines, the heathen nation which has wrongfully taken away the most glorious part of Israel's (or Verdopolis's) national life.

Even this is not the most degrading comparison: the phrase "cast in your lot with us" has its source in Proverbs 1;14, where it is said by a gang of thieves tempting an innocent young man. And "gone up from among us" may be a double echo, referring to I John 2:19, the voluntary separation of heretics from fellowship with the Church, as well as the Exodus. Charles Wellesley has succeeded in comparing the Angrians to the Israelites, the Philistines, thieves, and heretics, all in one paragraph — no mean feat of scurrility.

Clusters of Biblical allusions and quotations are common in *My Angria*. There *is* a long section with just one — chapter III in this edition. The Bible evidently affords no parallels to the speeches and gossip at a public meeting.

The next chapter makes up for it, however. Here, in a setting the narrator makes as regal as he can ("rich deep sombre hangings, dazzling carpets, and Tyrian couches"), exalted persons (the king and queen of Angria) enact a scene of exalted passions (love and statecraft). The descriptions and speeches should be exalted, too — grand, majestic, and in a high style. Thus we are given a profusion of Biblical phrases, striking in themselves, but often cut off from their Biblical contexts, like flowers in a vase. "He is ever the messenger of Satan," for example, certainly sounds dramatic, but gains little in meaning or resonance when we read it in its original setting of II Corinthians. Next to Charles Wellesley's use of scripture, it is curiously unimaginative. Given Zamorna's character, we could read it as another instance of irony, but that isn't Bronte's intention. We respond properly to this and other allusions in the scene by ignoring their Biblical contexts, and paying close attention instead to the association of stateliness and grandeur that the phrasing, diction, and rhythms of the Authorised Version had accumulated by this point in the history of the language. "Eat the bread and drink the waters of bitterness," for example, *sounds* as though it ought to be in the Authorised Version, but it is far enough from the three possible sources names in the notes to prove that she wasn't copying any of them.

One other Biblical echo in the scene is so distinctive it deserves its own comment. Brontë's source is one of the most affecting passages in St. John's gospel. As Mary stands weeping by the empty tomb, she sees a man she does not recognize. He asks her why she weeps.

> She, supposing him to be the gardener, saith unto him, Sir, if thou have borne him hence, tell me where thou hast laid him.... Jesus saith unto her, Mary. She ... saith unto him, Rabboni; which is to say, Master. (John 20:15b, 16,A.V.)

Now here is the supposed Major Albert presenting himself to Queen Mary Henrietta:

> Major Albert fixed on her a long and steadfast gaze. Ere he withdrew

> it she looked up and saw him.... For a moment she stood bewildered.... One word however - her own name, Mary, whispered in a low tone ... - sufficed to complete the recognition. She ... said softly and sadly, "Ah, Zamorna, did you think I could be blinded by a mask like that?" (32)

This parody of an episode in the Easter story has the effect of irreverence, especially considering the moral distance between Zamorna and the risen Christ. Yet the intention behind it is not irreverent. The Bible is a source of phrases and allusions, but also a story-book — for Charlotte, in fact, the greatest story-book. An immature poet imitates, said T.S. Eliot (182); and here she is simply trying to recreate, in her own dramatic situation, the powerful emotion produced in her by the passage from St. John.

The native exuberance of Charlotte Bronte's writing at eighteen show in her ad hoc use of the sources she loves, as well as in her wild variety of genres, voices, and moods in *My Angria*. She is not yet ready to turn "to a cooler region, where the dawn breaks grey and sober and the coming of day, for a time at least, is subdued in clouds" (Brontë, "Farewell" 47).

DOUGLAS LEWIS

WORKS CITED

Alexander, Christine. "Angria Revalued: Charlotte Brontë's Efforts to Free Herself From Her Juvenilia." *AUMLA* 53 (1980): 54-63.

———. *The Early Writings of Charlotte Brontë*. Oxford: Basil Blackwell, 1983.

———. "Art and Artists in Charlotte Brontë's Juvenilia." *Brontë Society Transactions* 20 (1991): 177-205.

Anderson, Benedict. *Imagined Communities: Reflections on the Origin and Spread of Nationalism*. 2nd ed. London and New York: Verso, 1991.

Blom, M.A. "Apprenticeship in 'The World Below': Charlotte Brontë's Juvenilia." *English Studies in Canada* 1 (1975): 290-303.

Brennan, Timothy. "The National Longing for Form." *Nation and Narration*. Homi K. Bhabba, ed. London and New York: Routledge, 1990.

Brontë, Charlotte. *The Twelve Adventurers: A Romantic Tale*. John Barach and others, eds. Edmonton: Juvenilia Press, 1993.

———. *An Edition of the Early Works of Charlotte Brontë*. Christine Alexander, ed. 2 vols. Oxford: Basil Blackwell, 1987-1991.

———. *Five Novelettes*. Winifred Gérin, ed. London: The Folio Press, 1971.

———. *Jane Eyre*. Margaret Smith, ed. Harmondsworth, Middlesex: Penguin, 1975.

———. *Shirley*. Andrew and Judith Hook, eds. Harmondsworth, Middlesex: Penguin Books, 1974.

———. *Villette*. Mark Lilly, oed. Hammondsworth, Middlesex: Penguin Books, 1979.

Brontë, Charlotte and Patrick Branwell. *The Miscellaneous and Unpublished Writings of Charlotte and P.B. Brontë*. Thomas James Wise and John Alexander Symington, eds. 2 vols. The Shakespeare Head Brontë. Oxford: Basil Blackwell, 1936-8.

———. *The Poems of Charlotte Brontë and Patrick Branwell Brontë*. Thomas James Wise and John Alexander Symington, eds. The Shakespeare Head Brontë. Oxford: Basil Blackwell, 1934.

Chapman, H.W. *The Last Tudor King*. New York: Macmillan Company, 1959.

Colley, Linda. *Britons: Forging the Nation 1701-1837*. New Haven and London: Yale University Press, 1992.

Cunnington, C. Willett and Phillis. *Handbook of English Costume in the Nineteenth Century*. London: Faber and Faber, 1959.

Debrett's Peerage and Baronetage. Charles Kidd and David Williamson, eds. London: Macmillan, 1990.

Eliot, T.S. *Selected Essays*. New York: Harcourt Brace, 1964.

Evans, Ivor H. *Brewer's Dictionary of Phrase and Fable*. Revised Ed. London: Cassell Ltd., 1981.

Foster, Vanda. *A Visual History of Costume: The Nineteenth Century*. London: BT Batsford, 1984.

Gaskell, Elizabeth. *The Life of Charlotte Brontë*. Angus Easson, ed. Oxford: Oxford University Press, 1996.

Gérin, Winifred. *The Brontës: The Formative Years*. Harlow: Longman Group, 1973.

Greer, Germaine. *Slip-shod Sybils: Recognition, Rejection, and the Woman Poet*. Harmondsworth, Middlesex: Penguin, 1995.

Johnson, Samuel. *A Dictionary of the English Language*. (1755) New York: Arno Press Inc., 1979.

L.E.L. (Letitia Elizabeth Landon). *The Venetian Bracelet, The Lost Pleiad, A History of the Lyre, and Other Poems*. London: Longman, Rees, Orme, Brown and Green, 1829.

Margetson, Stella. *Regency London*. London: Cassell & Company Ltd., 1971.

Meyer, Susan. "Colonialism and the Figurative Strategy of *Jane Eyre*." *Macropolitics of Nineteenth-Century Literature: Nationalism, Exoticism, Imperialism*. Jonathan Arac and Harriet Ritvo, eds. Philadelphia: University of Pennsylvania Press, 1991. 159-83.

Radcliffe, Ann. *The Romance of the Forest*. 3 vols. London: Printed for T. Hockham and J. Carpenter, New and Old Bond Street, 1791.

Sadie, Stanley, ed. *The New Grove Dictionary of Musical Instruments*. 3 vols. London: Macmillan, 1984.

Said, Edward W. *Orientalism*. New York: Vintage Books, 1979.

———. *Culture and Imperialism*. New York: Vintage Books, 1993.

Shorter, Clement. *The Brontës: Life and Letters*. 2 vols. New York: Haskell House Publishers Ltd., 1969.

Spencer, Edmund. *Travels in Circassia, Krim-Tartary, &c.* (1837). 2 vols. 3rd ed. London, 1839.

Thompson, Neville. *Wellington after Waterloo*. London: Routledge, 1986.

Wilks, Brian. *The Brontës*. New York: The Viking Press, 1975.

Williams, Meg Harris. "Book Magic: Aesthetic Conflicts in Charlotte Brontë's Juvenilia." *Nineteenth-Century Literature* 42 (1987): 29-45.

Williamson, James A. *A Short History of British Expansion.* 2 vols. 5th ed. London: Macmillan and Co. Ltd., 1964.

Zonana, Joyce. "The Sultan and the Slave: Feminist Orientalism and the Structure of *Jane Eyre.*" *Signs* 18 (1993): 592-617.

Juvenilia Press Catalogue

GENERAL EDITOR: Christine Alexander

Available volumes can be purchased via the Juvenilia Press website: www.arts.unsw.edu.au/juvenilia/

Volumes in the series:

- *Jack & Alice*, by Jane Austen at age c.13. Edited by Juliet McMaster and others. 1992, 1994.
- *The Twelve Adventurers: A Romance*, by Charlotte Brontë at 13. Edited by Juliet McMaster and others. 1993, 1994.
- *Amelia Webster and The Three Sisters*, by Jane Austen at c.13 and 16. Edited by Juliet McMaster and others. 1993, 1995.
- *Indamora to Lindamira*, by Lady Mary Pierrepont (later Wortley Montagu) at c.14. Edited by Isobel Grundy, with Susan Hillabold. 1994. First publication.
- *Norna, or The Witch's Curse*, by Louisa May Alcott at c.15. Edited by Juliet McMaster and others. 1994.
- *Pockets Full of Stars*, by Alison White from age 13. Edited by Arlette Zinck. 1994.
- *Branwell's Blackwoods Magazine*, by Branwell Brontë at 11. Edited by Christine Alexander, with Vanessa Benson. 1995. First publication.
- *The History of England*, by Jane Austen at 15. Edited by Jan Fergus and others. 1995, 2003.
- *Love and Freindship*, by Jane Austen at 14. Edited by Juliet McMaster and others. 1995, 2006, 2008.
- *Edward Neville*, by George Eliot at 14. Edited by Juliet McMaster and others. 1995. Revised edition, 2009.
- *Catharine, or The Bower*, by Jane Austen at 16. Edited by Juliet McMaster and others. 1996, 2005, 2011.

Juvenilia Press

Catalogue

- *Henry and Eliza*, by Jane Austen at c.13. Edited by Karen L. Hartnick and others. 1996, 2011.
- *A Quiet Game*, by Margaret Atwood at c.17. Edited by Kathy Chung and Sherrill Grace. 1997 (First publication), 2006.
- *The Young Visiters*, by Daisy Ashford at 9. Edited by Juliet McMaster and others. 1997. (not available for sale)
- *My Angria and the Angrians*, by Charlotte Brontë at 18. Edited by Juliet McMaster, Leslie Robertson and others. 1997, 2011.
- *Embryo Words*, by Margaret Laurence from age 14. Edited by Nora Foster Stovel and others. 1997.
- *A Collection of Letters*, by Jane Austen at c.16. Edited by Juliet McMaster and others. 1998, 2006, 2011.
- *Lesley Castle*, by Jane Austen at c.15. Edited by Jan Fergus and others. 1998, 2006, 2011.
- *Satan in a Barrel, and other early stories*, by Malcolm Lowry at 16. Edited by Sherrill Grace. 1999.
- *Evelyn*, by Jane Austen at 16. Edited by Peter Sabor and others. 1999.
- *Albion and Marina*, by Charlotte Brontë at 14. Edited by Juliet McMaster and others. 1999.
- *Colors of Speech*, by Margaret Laurence at 19-20. Edited by Nora Foster Stovel and others. 2000. First publication.
- *The Adventurer*, by Lady Mary Pierrepont (later Wortley Montagu) at 14. Edited by Isobel Grundy and others. 2000. First publication.
- *Tales of the Islanders, Volume 1*, by Charlotte Brontë at 13. Edited by Christine Alexander and others. 2001, 2006.

Juvenilia Press

Catalogue

- *Early Voices*, by Greg Hollingshead, Carol Shields, Aritha van Herk, and Ruby Wiebe. Edited by T.L. Walters and James King. 2001. First publication.
- *Jack & Alice*, by Jane Austen at c.13. Edited by Joseph Wiesenfarth, with Laura Maestrelli and Kristin Smith. 2001.
- *Peter Paul Rubens and Other Friendly Folk*, by Opal Whiteley, at 6-7. Edited by Laura Cappello, Juliet McMaster, Lesley Peterson, and Chris Wagner. 2001.
- *Tales of the Islanders, Volume 2*, by Charlotte Brontë at 13. Edited by Christine Alexander and others. 2002, 2006.
- *Sunbeams from a Golden Machine*, by Marian Engel at 16. Edited by Afra Kavanagh and Tammy MacNeil. 2002.
- *Frederic & Elfrida*, by Jane Austen at 11 or 12. Edited by Peter Sabor, Sylvia Hunt and Victoria Kortes-Papp. 2002.
- *Incidents from Phippy's Schooldays*, by Philip Larkin at c.15. Edited by Brenda Allen and James Acheson. 2002. First publication.
- *Tales of the Islanders, Volume 3*, by Charlotte Brontë at 14. Edited by Christine Alexander and others. 2003.
- *Artless Tales*, by Anna Maria Porter at 13. Edited by Leslie Robertson, Lesley Peterson, and Juliet McMaster. 2003. First publication since 1793.
- *The Three Sisters*, by Jane Austen at c.16. Edited by Joseph Wiesenfarth, Laura Maestrelli and Kristin Smith. 2004.
- *The Diary of Iris Vaughan*, written from age 7. Edited by Peter Alexander and Peter Midgley. 2004, 2010.
- *Tales of the Islanders, Volume 4*, by Charlotte Brontë at 14. Edited by Christine Alexander and others. 2005.

Juvenilia Press

Catalogue

- *Lady Susan*, by Jane Austen at c.18. Edited by Christine Alexander and David Owen. 2005, 2011.
- *Three Mini-Dramas*, by Jane Austen at c.12, 13 and 17. Edited by Juliet McMaster, Lesley Peterson and others. 2006.
- *Dick Doyle's Journal*, by Richard Doyle at 15. Edited by Juliet McMaster and others. 2006.
- *Jane Austen's Men*, by Jane Austen at c.12 to 14. Edited by Sylvia Hunt and others. 2007.
- *Dick Doyle's Journal, Volume 2*, by Richard Doyle at 15. Edited by Juliet McMaster and others. 2008.
- *The Rectory Magazine*, by Lewis Carroll at c.15. Edited by Valerie Sanders and Elizabeth O'Reilly. 2008.
- *The Gipsy Dancer & Early Poems*, by Dorothy Hewett at age 7–12. Edited by Christine Alexander and others. 2009.
- *Dick Doyle's Journal, Volume 3*, by Richard Doyle at 15-16. Edited by Juliet McMaster, Amy Stafford, and others. 2009.
- *The History of England & Cassandra's Portraits*, by Jane Austen at 15. Edited by Annette Upfal and Christine Alexander. 2009.
- *The Female Advocate*, by Sarah Fyge Egerton at 14-16. Edited by Peter Merchant, with Steven Orman. 2010.
- *The History of the Young Men*, by Patrick Branwell Brontë at 13. Edited by William Baker, with others. 2010.
- *The Early Tales*, by Mary Grant Bruce at 20. Edited by Pamela Nutt, with others. 2011.
- *Crossing Canada 1907: The Diary of Hope Hook*, by Hope Hook at 14. Edited by Juliet McMaster, with others. 2011.